IT'S AN OLD NEW ENGLAND CUSTOM

It's an Old New England Custom

EDWIN VALENTINE MITCHELL

THE VANGUARD PRESS, INC. · NEW YORK

Published simultaneously in Canada by the
Copp Clark Company, Ltd.

Designed by Stefan Salter
Manufactured in the United States of America by H. Wolff,
New York, N.Y.

To Jean Mitchell Boyd

CONTENTS

FOREWORD

Grateful acknowledgment is made to James M. Strong of Hartford, Connecticut, for helpful information. I am also indebted to a number of booksellers and librarians for aid in tracking down material, particularly to Miss Elva B. McCormick of Brentano's Bookshop, Hartford, Mrs. Lucy Gay Brown of the Huntting Bookshop in Springfield, Massachusetts, Miss Nada Kramar of Washington, D. C., and Mrs. Irene Jayne Smith, formerly reference librarian of the Hartford Public Library. Most of the research was done in the library of the Connecticut Historical Society, and my best thanks are due to Thompson Harlow, the librarian, and Miss Frances Hoxie, his assistant, for invaluable aid.

The reader should bear in mind that in old accounts New England towns which are spoken of as adjoining each other may now be separated by other towns that have since been carved from their flanks.

E. V. M.

IT'S AN OLD NEW ENGLAND CUSTOM

TO HAVE PIE FOR BREAKFAST

THAT fine old institution, the New England breakfast, is not what it was in the days when a man with an appetite could sit down to a table customarily laden with more good food than is now served at all meals of the day combined. Gone are the great juicy steaks, the red-hot chops, the vast platters of smoking ham and eggs, the hashed-brown potatoes, and the steaming stacks of buckwheat cakes brought on in relays and eaten with maple syrup from the Berkshires or the Green Mountains. All of the more substantial viands have been banished from the morning board, and with them into exile has gone that most exotic and traditional of all New England breakfast table dishes —pie.

Pie formerly graced Mr. Emerson's breakfast table at Concord in the days when New England was in bloom, as it also did that of Dr. Holmes, the amiable autocrat, poet, and professor of the breakfast table. Did he not say, "I will thank you to pass the pie, if you please?" Most New Englanders were too busy eating to do much talking at breakfast, but the consumption of a large wedge-shaped piece of pie did no more than put a temporary stop to the pleasant flow of Dr. Holmes's talk. At the Longfellow home in Cambridge, whenever a flake of piecrust fell into the beard of the author of "Excelsior," the poet's attention was called to its presence there by some member of the family remarking in the most casual and innocent way, "There's a gazelle in the garden." The remark was one which the Longfellows picked up from the wife of that splendidly bearded man, James T. Fields, the Boston publisher, whose literary breakfasts were noted for their distinguished company and blueberry cake.

In the Revolutionary period, when our forefathers got in some of their best work at the breakfast table, New England produced the biggest generals and other military officers in point of avoirdupois. This is shown by the following memorandum which was found in the pocketbook of an officer of the Massachusetts line.

August 19, 1783.

Weighed at the scales at West Point

General Washington	209 lbs.
General Knox	280
General Lincoln	224
General Huntington	132
General Greaton	166
Colonel Swift	219
Colonel Michael Jackson	252
Colonel Henry Jackson	238
Lieut.-Colonel Ebenezer Huntington	232
Lieut.-Colonel D. Cobb	186
Lieut.-Colonel D. Humphreys	221

What an eleven was here, and every man, with the exception of General Washington, was a New Englander! The combined weights of these officers, including the commander in chief, adds up to the impressive figure of 2,379 pounds. Subtracting General Washington's 209 pounds leaves 2,170 pounds, or an average for the ten New Englanders of 217 pounds per man. The mighty General Knox, who weighed in at 280 pounds and was therefore the heaviest of these heavyweights, fought in all the principal battles of the Revolution and was our first Secretary of War. He loved good food but had the misfortune to die at an untimely age of a chicken bone in his throat. Difficult to explain is the diminutive General Huntington, weighing only 132, who appears like a minnow among the whales. Evidently he was one of those unfortunate persons born without a tooth for pie, a man with no appetite for breakfast except in its most attenuated modern form.

Old tavern bills are often interesting as social documents because of the light they throw on the customs, habits, and manners of the people of bygone times. Take, for instance, the following bill which was paid by the Second Congregational Church of Hartford in 1784. A new minister was settled on the church that year, and the bill represents the cost to the parish of the ordination. It was a solemn occasion, but it was not without its cheerful side, as is evident from the items in the bill.

It is plain from this bill that three of the ministers came to town the day before, probably arriving in the evening, since there was no charge for supper, though they may have arrived earlier and

The South Society in Hartford,
to Israel Seymour, Dr.

1784		£	s.	d.
May 4th to keeping ministers, etc.				
" " "	2 mugs tody	0	2	4
" " "	5 segars	0	5	10
" " "	1 pint of wine	0	3	0
" " "	3 lodgings	0	0	9
May 5th "	3 bitters	0	0	9
" " "	3 breakfasts	0	3	6
" " "	15 boles of punch . . .	1	10	0
" " "	24 dinners	1	16	0
" " "	11 bottles wine	3	6	0
" " "	5 mugs flip	0	5	10
" " "	3 boles punch	0	6	0
" " "	3 boles of tody	0	3	6

Received by me,
Israel Seymour.

been privately entertained that evening. In any case, before retiring at the inn, each had a night-cap, two of them drinking a mug of toddy apiece, the third a bottle of wine, and between them they smoked five cigars costing one shilling tuppence each. The cigars seem rather an extravagance at that price, particularly when it is remembered that native cigars made by the wives of Connecticut Valley farmers sold then for only a penny each and were usually free to guests at inns. But as these local cigars were admittedly pretty rank, the godly gentlemen cannot perhaps be blamed for ordering the best the house afforded in the way of the imported article from Havana. Ordinations, moreover, were times of abundant hospitality, with everything on the parish, at least so far as the visiting clergy were concerned. The beds were cheap at threepence each, and the charge for the three bitters taken before breakfast and for the meal itself was not excessive. That the breakfast was a substantial one may be deduced from the fact that it cost only a few pence less than the dinner. From the other items it is reasonable to conclude that the reverend companions became quite tipsy, but there was nothing unusual in this. It was one of the quaint customs of the time.

Breakfast was not the same everywhere in New England. More fish, for example, was used along the seaboard than in the hinterland, but even on Cape Cod they had pie for breakfast, as is shown by the following bill of fare of the inhabitants of that region from a description of the town of Chatham printed in 1802.

"Food can so easily be procured, either on the shore or in the sea, that, with the profit which arises from their voyages, in which it must be confessed they labor very hard, the people are enabled to cover their tables well with provisions. A breakfast among the inhabitants, and even among those who are called the poorest, for there are none which may be called really poor, consists of tea or coffee, brown bread, generally with butter, sometimes without, salt or fresh fish, fried or broiled. A dinner affords one or more of the following dishes: roots and herbs; salted beef or pork boiled; fresh butcher's meat not more than twelve times a year; wild fowl frequently in the autumn and winter; fresh fish boiled or fried with pork; shell fish; salt fish boiled; Indian pudding; pork baked with beans. Tea or coffee also frequently constitutes part of the dinner. A supper consists of tea or coffee, and fish, as at breakfast; cheese, cakes made of flour, gingerbread, and pies of several sorts. This bill of fare will serve, with little variation, for all the fishing towns in the county. *In many families there is no difference between breakfast and supper; cheese, cakes, and pies being common at the one as at the other.*"

Half a century later when Thoreau and his friend, Ellery Channing, visited Cape Cod, they put up one night with an old oysterman of Wellfleet, who in the morning provided them with substantially the same kind of breakfast. Thoreau's brief account of this meal is interesting and amusing.

"Before sunrise the next morning they let us out

again, and I ran over to the beach to see the sun come out of the ocean. The old woman of eighty-four winters was already out in the cold morning wind, bareheaded, tripping about like a young girl, and driving up the cow to milk. She got the breakfast with dispatch, and without noise or bustle; and meanwhile the old man resumed his stories, standing before us, who were sitting, with his back to the chimney, and ejecting his tobacco-juice right and left into the fire behind him, without regard to the dishes that were there preparing. At breakfast we had eels, buttermilk cake, cold bread, green beans, doughnuts, and tea. . . . I ate of the apple-sauce and the doughnuts, which I thought had sustained the least detriment from the old man's shots, but my companion refused the apple-sauce, and ate of the hot cake and green beans, which had appeared to me to occupy the safest part of the hearth. But on comparing notes afterward, I told him that the buttermilk cake was particularly exposed, and I saw how it suffered repeatedly, and therefore I avoided it; but he declared that, however that might be, he witnessed that the apple-sauce was seriously injured, and had therefore declined that."

After breakfast they filled their pockets with doughnuts, which the old oysterman was pleased to find they called by the same name that he did, and, paying for their entertainment, took their departure. It was perhaps an oversight that they were not offered pie for breakfast, but at least they did have doughnuts, which still happily survive on many New England breakfast tables. The most remarkable thing about the meal was the manner of its preparation. In mid-nineteenth century it was cooked before an open fire.

The memorableness of a breakfast may depend on the circumstances in which it was eaten, or the food it consisted of, or both. A breakfast memorable on both counts was served to an English traveler named John Lambert in a Vermont farmhouse on the shore of Lake Champlain at the beginning of the last century. Lambert gives an account of it in his book, *Travels in Lower Canada and North America in the Years* 1806, 1807, *and* 1808, which was published in London in 1810. On his passage up the lake, Lambert was forced to land early in the morning, after a trying night on the water. Tired, cold, and hungry, he applied at a farmhouse for food. Here is the story of his reception.

"We were nearly two hours before we could get the vessel off the rocks. At length having succeeded, we coasted along the shore, until four o'clock in the morning, when we arrived in a small bay in the township of Shelburne, about sixty miles from St. John's, situated in the widest part of the lake. Here we went ashore at the first farmhouse, at a little distance from the bay. The door was only on the latch, and we entered; but the people were not yet up. Having awakened the master of the house, and told him our situation, he said we were welcome, and that he would get up immediately. In the meantime, we collected some wood, and, putting it upon the live embers in the fire place, soon made a large fire. This was a most comfortable relief, after the cold night we had passed on board our miserable sloop. We found that a considerable quantity of snow had fallen in this part of the lake, though we had not met any during the passage.

"The master of the house, with two of his sons, were soon up, and, having put the kettle on the fire, made preparations for breakfast. About six o'clock, his wife and daughters, two pretty little girls, came into the kitchen, where we were assembled, and in the course of half an hour we had the pleasure of sitting down to a substantial American breakfast, consisting of eggs, fried pork, beefsteaks, apple-tarts, pickles, cheese, cider, tea, and toast dipped in melted butter and milk. We were surprised at seeing such a variety of eatables, as it was not a tavern; but the farmer was a man of property, and carried on the farming business to a considerable extent. He showed us a great number of cheeses of his own making; and, for churning butter, he had made a kind of half barrel, with a place for one of his young boys to sit astride as on horseback. This machine moving up and down answered the double purpose of a churn for making butter, and a rocking horse for his children.

"Having made an excellent breakfast, we inquired of our worthy host what we had to pay. He said he should be satisfied with a York shilling (about 7d. sterling); this however we considered too small a sum for the trouble we had given him and his family, and the handsome manner in which he had entertained us; we therefore gave him a quarter of a dollar each, that being the tavern price for breakfast. We then took our leave, and went on board our vessel, equally pleased with the disinterested hospitality of the American farmer, as with the comfortable refreshment we had received at his house."

The oddest item in this Vermont breakfast is the cider, but at that time and for many years thereafter it was drunk at all times of the day in New England, and commonly at breakfast. In ordinary seasons it was worth about a dollar a barrel. It was usually drawn in a mug or bowl, and among farmers it was considered a breach of manners not to offer it to any casual visitor or traveler. It was intoxicating, but was seldom taken in quantities sufficient to intoxicate—at least, not at breakfast.

President John Adams was in the habit of tossing off a quart tankard of hard cider before breakfast, and it did not seem to do him any harm, as he lived to be ninety.

Another breakfast memorable for the circumstances in which it was eaten as well as the food comprising it was the one consumed at No. 92 Second Street, Fall River, Massachusetts, on a swelteringly hot August day in the year 1892, by Andrew J. Borden, his second wife, Abby L. D. Borden, and a guest at the house, the brother of Mr. Borden's first wife, John V. Morse. The breakfast, probably the most hideous in New England annals, consisted of mutton soup, warmed over mutton, johnnycake, coffee, and cookies. This horrid meal was eaten by the three persons mentioned about seven o'clock on the morning of August fourth. Two hours later Mr. Borden's daughter, Lizzie, came downstairs and, declining the breakfast upon which her parents and uncle had regaled themselves, contented herself with half a cup of coffee and part of a cookie. It was a breakfast, says Edmund Pearson, well adapted to set the stage for a tragedy. And, as everybody knows, a tragedy was enacted in the house that same morning. Within the space of about two hours after Lizzie came down to breakfast, Mr. and Mrs. Borden were corpses, hacked to death with a hatchet. Today, more than fifty years after these notorious murders, people still get cold shivers reading about the warm mutton broth eaten for breakfast on that hot August day in Fall River.

A universal geography is scarcely the kind of work in which one would expect to find information concerning the food and drink taken by New Englanders for breakfast, and yet that is precisely what one does find in Samuel G. Goodrich's *Pictorial Geography of the World*, published in Boston in 1841. "The breakfast," says Mr. Goodrich in the section of his work devoted to New England, "which, in the country, is held at an early hour, and often by sunrise, is no evanescent thing. In a farmer's family, it consists of little less than ham, beef, sausages, bread, butter, boiled potatoes, pies, coffee, and cider. The use of coffee in the morning, and of tea at night, is almost universal. At hotels and boarding houses, the standing breakfast is of beef, mutton, ham, broiled chickens, sausages, tripe, various kinds of fish, tongue, bread, butter, coffee, and cider."

But Charles Dickens, who was more conscious of food than most authors, was not favorably impressed with the meals served to him at the Boston hotel where he stayed when he visited this country the year following the publication of Mr. Goodrich's geography. "In our private room," he says in

American Notes for General Circulation, "the cloth could not, for any earthly consideration, have been laid for dinner without a huge glass dish of cranberries in the middle of the table; and breakfast would have been no breakfast unless the principal dish were a deformed beefsteak with a great flat bone in the centre, swimming in hot butter, and sprinkled with the very blackest of all possible pepper."

This is an unkind judgment, but not so many years later Mark Twain, who lived a great part of his life and did his best work in New England, described with equal candor the beefsteak he had for breakfast on Dickens's side of the Atlantic. He said it was neither cut right nor cooked properly. It came on the table in a small pewter platter bordered with grease-soaked potatoes. It was the size, shape, and thickness of a man's hand with the thumb and fingers cut off. It was overdone, rather dry, tasted pretty insipid, aroused no enthusiasm.

Then with the memory of hundreds of New England breakfasts in mind, Mark Twain wrote a description of the kind of beefsteak he might have had for breakfast at home. It is the most mouthwatering description in literature. "A mighty porterhouse steak an inch and a half thick, hot and sputtering from the griddle; enriched with little melting bits of butter of the most unimpeachable freshness and genuineness; the precious juices of the meat trickling out and joining with the gravy, archipelagoed with mushrooms; a township or two of tender, yellowish fat gracing an outlying district of this ample county of beefsteak; the long white bone which divides the sirloin from the tenderloin still in its place."

To this magnificent breakfast steak Mark Twain added a great cup of American homemade coffee, with the cream afroth on the top, some real butter, firm and yellow and fresh, some smoking hot biscuits, and a plate of buckwheat cakes with transparent syrup. In short, the kind of breakfast to which New Englanders were accustomed.

The seasons were not without their influence on the New England breakfast. Buckwheat cakes, thin and crisp around the edges, were considered suitable only for a winter morning, as were also baptist cakes. Oatmeal, which had simmered on the stove all night and it would have been sacrilege to call porridge, was supposed to heat the blood, so many persons did not eat it in summer. According to *The Epicure*, published by the famous New England grocery house of S. S. Pierce and Company of Boston, the ladies of Beacon Hill in the late sixties found the following dishes suitable for breakfast in autumn and winter: stewed pigeons with mushrooms, deviled gizzards, liver pudding, pork cheese, hashed poultry, minced veal, hash balls, game birds, venison pasty, tongue or ham toast, rice cakes, sausages, fish cakes, and broiled tomatoes. Norwegian salt mackerel was a favorite breakfast dish with some men. But many families stuck to the same breakfast the year round. One family I knew never deviated winter or summer from hash and pancakes.

Codfish cakes, brown and crisp and fluffy, are still a Sunday morning tradition in many New England families, especially in the vicinity of Boston, since breakfast on that day is usually a more leisurely affair than on weekdays. When the English poet and critic, Matthew Arnold, came to this country to lecture and was confronted with fish cakes for breakfast, he is reported to have remarked to a table companion, "Try one of these buns. They're not so bad as they look."

Matthew Arnold came here for the first time in 1883. He wisely refrained from writing a book about America, but in his letters home he had a good deal to say about the country in general and American food in particular. He was too kind a man to criticize our diet, but he did view it with surprise, and occasionally with alarm. In Boston he had a great dinner of venison and champagne with Phillips Brooks. The next day he left for Amherst to lecture. Here he stayed at the president's house, where he had to get up at half past five to catch a train. The president's three daughters breakfasted with him. "A porridge made of split oat groats," he writes, "which I am beginning to like (one takes it with cream), a roll and a cup of tea did very well for me. There was an immense beef steak, but that was too much for me so early."

A few days later he was at Andover, Massachusetts. "Called at seven," he reports, "breakfast with a party of professors and their wives—coffee, fruit, fishballs, potatoes, hashed veal, and mince-pies, with rolls and butter." When Arnold's letters were published posthumously a dozen years later, a cry went up from Andover. The pie was absolutely denied. Neither mince nor any other kind of pie, it was protested, was served for breakfast at Andover when Mr. Arnold was there. The poet perhaps had in mind some other New England breakfast he had recently eaten, and credited the pie to the wrong place, or maybe there were pancakes that morning which he mistook for pies. Large-scale pancakes were not unknown in New England in the days of spacious breakfasts. In any case, it is amusing to think of the professors years later making a *casus belli* of mince pie.

By the time Arnold's letters were published in the mid-nineties, pie for breakfast was rapidly going out of fashion, along with almost everything else on the morning menu. Why was this? During the last decades of the last century more and more Americans went abroad, and it was these travelers who brought home the idea of the Continental breakfast, consisting of nothing but a hard, cold roll and a cup of coffee. It became fashionable to denounce pie as provincial. No one who wished to be thought sophisticated dared eat a big breakfast. One must do as they did in Paris—not Paris, Maine, but Paris, France—and conform to the Continental standard, low as it was. Instead of converting the Parisians to pie, these innocents abroad permitted themselves to be seduced into surrendering their birthright. It is a conspicuous historical fact that nations are apt to copy each other's worst features rather than their best.

The anti-pie crusade was helped by the increasing tempo of American life. The curious notion that the more we rushed about the more civilized we were was beginning to take root. When we began to measure our progress by the rate of speed at which we could move and began to think that because we could get around ten or a dozen times faster than our grandfathers we were that much better than they were, pie as a morning dish was doomed. For nobody had time to eat a decent breakfast.

The female figure, too, may have had something to do with it, or rather men's ideas concerning the female figure. When pie was in vogue, the buxom figure was admired. Matrons were expected to look matronly. Women could afford to let themselves go in the matter of food, helping themselves to pie at any meal they wished without giving it a second thought. But with the gradual change in ideas of feminine beauty, women were obliged to consider the consequences of heavy eating. They began to cut down on food to reduce their figures, and breakfast, the first meal of the day, was the first to suffer. It was whittled down until it became nothing but an empty mockery of a meal.

Pie, however, continued to linger for some time on many New England breakfast tables. Journeying toward the White Mountains one summer at the close of the last century, Charles Dudley Warner fancied that he could draw a diet line passing through Bellows Falls and bending a little south on either side, which would mark, northward, the region of perpetual pie. But he came to the conclusion that pie was perhaps a matter of altitude rather than latitude, as he found that all the hill and country towns were full of women who would have felt ready to sink in mortification through their scoured kitchen floors if visitors caught them without a pie in the house. The absence of pie would have been more noticeable, he declared, than a scarcity of the Bible.

Since then, of course, pie has almost completely vanished from the breakfast tables of New England. Only occasionally is it to be encountered, and then in the most remote places. In the winter of 1940, I visited Criehaven off the Maine coast. It is a tiny fishing port on one of New England's farthest flung islands. My host, entering the kitchen in the morning, gazed for a moment at what his wife had set out for our breakfast, and then, "God bless my soul," he cried, "no pie!" But he was mistaken, for there was pie, and a memorable breakfast we made of it. There was oatmeal and toast and coffee, lobster stew and custard pie. It was the best stew I ever ate, and the custard pie just melted down my throat.

More recently, at Gouldsborough, Maine, a relative of mine was served black pumpkin pie for breakfast, which he said was delicious. Also on the table was a splendid chocolate cake.

But why, people ask, did New Englanders formerly eat so much for breakfast? The answer is quite simple. It was because they had great things to do.

TO SERVE TURKEY AND CRANBERRY SAUCE

THANKSGIVING has, of course, always been the time *par excellence* for food in New England, with roast turkey the traditional *pièce de résistance* of the feast. Even the Puritans forgot their fear of sensualism at Thanksgiving, abandoning themselves with gusto to the pleasures of the table, though there were times when the country was a desert island for food, and the colonists, like castaways, were in no danger of overeating.

There seems, however, to have been an abundance of provender at the first Pilgrim Thanksgiving at Plymouth in 1621, which was not an affair of a single day, but lasted a whole week, and, contrary to what many persons think, was without any religious significance. It was simply a period of relaxation and recreation following the gathering of the first harvest.

Yet it could hardly have been a time of rest for the four women of the colony upon whom fell the burden of preparing the food for the week's festivities. There were only fifty-five English left in Plymouth at the time, but Chief Massasoit stalked in at the head of ninety braves, and these friendly redskins were entertained by the whites for three days. The Indians for their part contributed venison to the communal larder. As the quartet of colonial dames, assisted by a servant and some young Puritan maids, slaved to feed the six score men, the smell of the meat roasting over the open fires must have been good.

It is safe to say that enormous quantities of food were consumed, because the Indians were born gluttons capable of tumbling more victuals into themselves than anyone would think humanly possible; and the colonial men present, if one may judge by the inherited capacity of some of their descendants, likewise gave a satisfactory account of themselves. Anyhow, the shooting was good around Plymouth that fall, so there was plenty of food for all. This we know from a letter which Edward Winslow wrote to a friend in England on December 11, 1621, in which he said:

"Our harvest being gotten in, our governor sent four men on fowling that so we might after a special manner rejoice together after we had gathered the fruits of our labors. They four killed as much fowl as with a little help beside served the company about a week. At which time among other recreations we exercised our arms, many of the Indians coming amongst us, and among the rest their greatest king Massasoyt with some ninety men, whom for three days we entertained and feasted, and they went out and killed five deer which they brought and bestow'd on our governor, and upon the captains and others."

It is a pleasant picture which Winslow sketches of the Pilgrims at play after a year of unspeakable trials and hardships on the edge of the wilderness. Here is no group of long-faced men and women taking their pleasures sadly, but a lively band of people in holiday mood, indulging in feasting and in their favorite sports and pastimes.

Since Governor Bradford mentioned that "beside waterfoule ther was great store of wild turkies" that fall, we may be certain that the men he sent out to make provision for the feast succeeded in bagging enough unsuspecting turkeys to make the tables groan.

Other writers of the period have told of the great flocks of wild turkeys that inhabited the oak and chestnut forests of New England. So common were they that in the 1730's dressed wild turkeys sold for only a penny and a half a pound in western Massachusetts. The price, of course, increased as the wild turkey population decreased, and by the close of the eighteenth century they were bringing fourpence per pound. In 1820, when these great game birds were rapidly vanishing, the price had risen to twelve and a half cents a pound and it became less common to see wild turkey wings used as hearth brushes in New England homes.

There is a delightful chapter in Brillat-Savarin's classic work on dining, *Physiologie du Goût*, in which the famous French gastronomist tells how he shot a wild turkey near Hartford, Connecticut, in the autumn of 1794. A refugee from the French Revolution, Brillat-Savarin while staying at Hartford was invited by an old farmer who lived in the backwoods to come and have some shooting. The farmer promised partridges, gray squirrels, and wild turkeys. Accordingly, one fine day in October the Frenchman and a friend, mounted on two hacks, rode out some five leagues from Hartford. Reaching their journey's end toward evening, they sat down in the farmhouse to an abundantly supplied supper table. "There was a superb piece of corned beef, a stewed goose, and a magnificent leg of mutton, with vegetables of every description, and at each end of the table two large jugs of cider."

The next day they went shooting, killing some plump partridges first, then knocking over six or seven gray squirrels, and finally their lucky star brought them into the middle of a flock of wild turkeys, which rose one after the other at short intervals, flying noisily and screaming loudly. The last and laziest bird rose only ten paces from Brillat-Savarin, who promptly brought it down. He and his friend took the partridges, the squirrels, and the turkey back to Hartford, where the celebrated gourmet arranged a little dinner for some of his American friends, at which the wings of the partridges were served *en papillottes* and the gray squirrels stewed in Madeira.

"As for the turkey, which was the only roast we had, it was charming to look upon, delightful to smell, and delicious to taste; and so, until the last morsel was eaten, you could hear all around the table, 'Very good! Exceedingly good!' 'Oh, my dear Sir, what a glorious bit!' "

It is not known where in the vicinity of Hartford Brillat-Savarin shot his wild turkey, but it may have been among the Turkey Hills of East Granby, which are the same distance from Hartford that Brillat-Savarin says he traveled, and, as the name indicates, were once a haunt of the noble bird. A few years later there were no wild turkeys left in Connecticut, for the last specimen was recorded shot there in 1813.

By the end of the eighteenth century the wild turkeys of New England, which had been retreating steadily westward, reached the line of the Connecticut River, where they made their last stand. There were flocks of them in the Berkshires and the mountainous regions of Vermont and among the hills of the Connecticut Valley. In the lifetime of the writer's grandparents there were still wild turkeys around Mount Holyoke and Mount Tom. During the winter of 1850-51 the last one was shot on Mount Tom. A turkey killed on Mount Holyoke in 1863 is thought to have been a fugitive from a barnyard.

Before the wild species was exterminated they sometimes visited their civilized relatives of the barnyard. In the mating season a wild turkey cock would fly in and strut and gobble and fight the domestic cock for the favors of the females. The wild gobbler always won, and in this way the domestic species was invigorated and kept up to scratch.

The old New England expression "to talk turkey" was coined in New Hampshire some time before 1846, when an Indian and a white man who had been hunting together came to divide the spoils, which consisted of a crow and a turkey. The white man, who was anxious to have the turkey, but wished to appear to make a fair division, said, "You take the crow and I'll take the turkey, or I'll take the turkey and you take the crow." The Indian grunted and replied, "Why you no talk turkey to me?"

In the olden times the New England housewife never had to worry about the Thanksgiving turkey being too large to fit her oven because she cooked it over an open fire. Families were larger then, and big birds favored. But the oven problem brought about an unusual Thanksgiving innovation just before the festival of 1945. This was the sale of split turkeys occasioned by the great number of extraordinarily large birds coming into the market. Raised to meet the requirements of the armed forces, these birds were released for civilian consumption as a result of the sudden end of the war. Marketmen, knowing that many housewives had ovens too small to accommodate such whopping birds, split the oversize turkeys in two, and the housewives, agreeing that half a turkey was better than none, bought the bisected birds, although they were uncertain how to prepare half a bird for the table and were apprehensive that it might dry unduly while cooking. All apparently turned out well, but in the future smaller turkeys will probably be the rule.

It is quite fitting that most of the cranberries which are made into sauce and eaten with turkey on Thanksgiving Day should come from New England, where the custom of serving cranberry sauce originated. The berry had existed in a wild state along New England shores since long before the coming of the Pilgrims, who, because the white blossom and stem bore a fancied resemblance to the head and neck of a crane, called it the craneberry. It still grows wild along the coast, not only on the mainland, but on the coastal islands as well. The Cranberry Islands off the Maine coast near Mount Desert were named from the abundance of wild cranberries found growing there.

The cultivated berry as we know it today is largely a product of Cape Cod. It was not until the days of sail were on the wane that the inhabitants of the Cape became interested in growing anything in the wastes of sand which reminded travelers of the deserts of Arabia. Obliged to cast about for a new means of livelihood, they began to cultivate the cranberry. A Cape resident had noticed that the vines around and over which the sand had drifted bore the best berries, and from this simple observation the modern cranberry industry was developed. The old salts of Cape Cod financed many of their cranberry bogs in the same way they financed the building of their ships, by splitting the cost into sixty-four parts and selling interests in a bog as they had sold shares in a vessel. These cranberry shares have often been held in the same family for generations. Today the cranberry bogs of Cape Cod produce three-fourths of the world's supply of the red berry with the tart taste.

Pie, especially pumpkin pie, was considered as essential to the old-fashioned New England Thanksgiving dinner as turkey and cranberry sauce. A want of molasses with which to make pies was more than once the cause of a New England town postponing its observance of the day. Once at Newbury, Vermont, when the minister read the Thanksgiving proclamation, a worthy deacon, who was not unmindful of the earthly pleasure to be derived from a good dinner, rose and said that as there was no molasses in town and his boys had gone to Charlestown, New Hampshire, to get some, he would move that Thanksgiving be postponed a week. When the boys did not return, the day was put off again, until finally the people of Newbury had to go without their molasses, and, since there was no "sweetning," presumably also without the customary pumpkin pies. One can only guess what happened to the boys. Similarly, at Colchester, Connecticut, the celebration of Thanksgiving was delayed a week beyond the appointed day because a sloop from New York with a hogshead of molasses for pies failed to arrive.

The New England governors in colonial times were not above using their annual Thanksgiving Day proclamations for purposes of political propaganda. Not only did they bid the people give thanks for the bounties of nature, but also for wise and beneficent laws effectively administered and for other blessings of good government. People who considered such political statements gross exaggerations or inventive reporting were thrown into a trampling rage, and ministers delivering Thanksgiving sermons in unheated meetinghouses would sometimes give an offending governor a thorough raking over the coals.

An amusing account of a public dinner given in 1714, at which bear meat and venison were eaten, has come down to us from the pen of the Rev. Lawrence Conant of Danvers, Massachusetts, who was evidently not averse to eating game that had been killed on the Sabbath.

"When ye services at ye meeting house were ended," he wrote, "ye council and other dignitaries were entertained at ye house of Mr. Epes, on ye hill near by, and we had a bountiful Thanksgiving dinner with bear's meat and venison, the last of which was a fine buck, shot in ye woods near by. Ye bear was killed in Lynn woods near Reading.

"After ye blessing was craved by Mr. Garrick of Wrentham, word came that ye buck was shot on ye Lord's day by Pequot, an Indian, who came to Mr. Epes with a lye in his mouth like Ananias of old.

"Ye council therefore refused to eat ye venison, but it was afterward decided that Pequot should receive 40 stripes save one, for lying and profaning ye Lord's day, restore Mr. Epes ye cost of ye deer, and considering this a just and righteous sentence on ye sinful heathen, and that a blessing had been craved on ye meat, ye council all partook of it but Mr. Shepard, whose conscious was tender on ye point of ye venison."

At Norwich, Connecticut, it was once the practice to celebrate Thanksgiving not only by eating turkey and cranberry sauce, but by lighting bonfires. In 1792 a young man was killed during the celebration.

"On Thursday evening last," says a newspaper account, "a young man by the name of Cook, aged 19, was instantly killed in this town by the discharge of a swivel. The circumstances, as near as we can recollect, were as follows:—In celebration of the day, (being Thanksgiving), a large number of boys had assembled, and by pillaging dry casks from the stores, wharves, &c. had erected a bonfire on the hill back of the Landing, and to make their rejoicings more sonorious, fired a swivel several times; at last a foolish fondness for a loud report, induced them to be pretty lavish of their powder—the explosion burst the swivel into a multitude of pieces, the largest of which, weighing about seven pounds, passed through the body of the deceased, carrying with it his heart, and was afterwards found in the street 30 or 40 rods from the place where it was fired.—While the serious lament the accident, they entertain a hope that good may come of evil, that the savage practice of making bonfires on the evening of Thanksgiving, may be exchanged for some other mode of rejoicing, more consistent with the genuine spirit of Christianity."

But this local custom of lighting bonfires on Thanksgiving Day continued in Norwich throughout the era of wooden barrels, or down to about the year 1925.

"They were touched off Thanksgiving morning," a man from Norwich told me, who as a boy had participated in these celebrations. "There were bonfires on all the seven hills of Norwich on Thanksgiving Day."

Thanksgiving did not immediately become a fixed annual festival in New England after the first Pilgrim observance, but it made headway steadily. It proved popular because it was a substitute for the festival of Christmas, which the Puritans had banished. It was as if they said, "If we can't have Christmas, we'll have our own feast." The idea of a Thanksgiving Day for the Lord's bounties gradually spread throughout the country until this old New England custom became a national one.

TO EAT CHEESE

THE town of Goshen, high up among the Litchfield hills, is the most elevated township in Connecticut. It is a land flowing with milk and honey, a rich grazing country, which was long and justly celebrated for the quantity and quality of the cheese it supplied to the pie-laden breakfast tables of the region. The town, it is said, can rightfully claim the distinction of having the first cheese factory in America.

Goshen was renowned not only for the cheese it produced in summer but also for the depth and long continuance of its snows in winter. While there would seem to be no connection between the two, it was the severity of the Goshen winters that gave the cheese industry its greatest impetus. For when Alexander Norton found that he could not stand the rigorous climate of Goshen, but must spend the winter in the South, he decided, as a thrifty Yankee, to see if he could not defray the expenses of his southern sojourn by taking along some good Goshen cheese to sell.

Accordingly, he bought several thousand pounds, which he succeeded in transporting safely to the South. This in itself was something of a feat, as boxing cheese or packing it in casks was unheard of then. Whether the journey was made by land or sea is uncertain, but as the year was 1792, it seems highly probable that Alexander Norton took passage in some coaster southward bound out of Bridgeport, or some other neighboring port, though, of course, like the tin peddlers of Connecticut, he may have taken his cargo of cheese south by horse marine. The New England peddlers, by the way, were said to have sold wooden nutmegs, basswood hams, and white oak cheeses. In any case, the experiment proved successful, and a new market was opened for Goshen cheese never before dreamed of in that hilltop town, though cheese is supposed to promote dreams.

Alexander Norton continued his southern cheese trading on an increasing scale for the next fifteen or twenty years, contracting in summer for his winter supply. He had wood cut and casks made to a pattern that would fit his cheese, a practice in which he is said to have been the pioneer. Afterward, he had some round boxes made, like the cheese containers in later use, and these are declared to have been the first cheese boxes.

There were certain tricks of the cheese trade that Alexander Norton was not slow to learn. At first he sold only white cheese, but soon discovered that colored cheese sold better. So he began to make what he called painted cheese, which he found he could sell readily for fifteen cents a pound, while the most he could get for the white was ten cents. The two were identical in quality, but people were under the impression that the painted cheese was English.

Alexander Norton's wife was the first person in Goshen to use annatto to color cheese, rubbing it through a cloth into the milk. The annatto gave it the same color as the cheese made in Gloucestershire, England. New England housewives were adepts in the art of doctoring cheese, often medicating it with sage, tansy, pennyroyal, balm, and other plants, which sometimes gave it an uncommon tinge, depending on the kind and amount of plant juice used. Various kinds of sage cheese are still made in New England, where it is supposed to be a peculiarly Yankee product. In its orthodox form it is a green cheese, like that of which the moon is reputed to be made, though the color apparently comes not from the sage, which is merely used for flavoring, but from the juice of spinach leaves and other plants mixed with the milk. It usually comes into the market in March and April.

In this connection there are some interesting hints to housewives on the buying and keeping of cheese in Amelia Simmons' *American Cookery*, which was published at Hartford in 1796. This little work—it is a pamphlet of forty-eight pages—is credited with being the first American cookbook. Old cookbooks often contain rather terrifying recipes, but those in Miss Simmons' work seem to be quite sensible and harmless. Of cheese she says, "The red smooth moist coated, and tight pressed, square edged Cheese, are better than white coat, hard rinded, or bilged; the inside should be yellow and flavored to your taste. Old shelves which have been only wiped down for years, are preferable to scoured and washed shelves. Deceits are used by salt petering the outside, or coloring with hemlock, cocumberries, or safron, infused into the milk; the taste of either supercedes every possible evasion."

Probably the publication of Miss Simmons' cookbook had no connection with the visit to Hartford the preceding year of Brillat-Savarin, the French gastronomist and culinary writer, who made the famous remark, "Desert without cheese is like a pretty girl with only one eye."

Before 1850 the manufacture of cheese was a home industry conducted chiefly by women. New England was then principally an agricultural region, and it was part of the weekly routine on nearly every farm. At least twice a week in summer quantities of butter and cheese were made, the women priding themselves on the quality of their dairy products quite as much as they did on the excellence of their pies and cakes. Recipes for making cheese were handed down in New England families from one generation to the next. Originally brought to this country by the colonists, these recipes were put to use as soon as herds to produce the curds had been established. No cheese-making equipment appears in the inventories of the first estates, but it was not long before it began to appear in the probate records.

Most farms had a special cheese house or cheese room, where were kept the clumsy press and the other paraphernalia used in making cheese and a cupboard or open shelves where the cheeses were placed to ripen. Although Miss Simmons recommended unscoured shelves, every precaution was taken in the way of cleanliness to prevent the cheese from becoming maggoty. On cheese-making days the polished wooden bowls and rows of shining pans were set out in the sunshine, and with much method and little bustle the skillful New England dairywomen cut the tender curds and went through the other steps involved in the process of manufacture in a way that made what might have been drudgery in other hands seem like a pastime. The sour juices that came trickling from the press when the curds were placed in the hoop for pressing gave the cheese room a distinct and pervasive odor of its own.

But to return to the land of Goshen. Spurred by the enterprise of Alexander Norton, other Goshenites began trading in cheese, and the Goshen product became well and widely known and the town the most prosperous farming community in Connecticut. An old account says that for neatness in and around their houses and in the appearance of general comfort and well-being the inhabitants of Goshen were unsurpassed by the people of any other town in the state. In 1801, the cheese made in Goshen amounted to 270,000 pounds.

The first pineapple cheeses were made in Goshen

in 1808 by Lewis Norton, who was granted a patent for the form he devised for making them. He kept fifty cows and made cheese from his own herd until 1843, when he began to purchase curds from neighboring dairymen and established the first cheese factory. His son, who migrated to New York State, built a cheese works there. It was the migrating Yankee who carried the art of cheese-making westward to New York, Ohio, Wisconsin, and beyond.

In 1845, Litchfield County, where Goshen is situated, produced 2,750,000 pounds of cheese, and in 1850 Connecticut led all the states of the Union in the amount of cheese produced per cow. Statistics from the census of 1850 show that the nine top-ranking states were Connecticut with sixty-two pounds of cheese per cow, Vermont fifty-nine, Massachusetts fifty-four, New York fifty-three, Ohio thirty-six, New Hampshire thirty-one, New Jersey thirty, Maine eighteen, and Rhode Island eleven. Vermont produced more cheese than all other states put together except Maine, New Hampshire, Massachusetts, Connecticut, Ohio, and New York, and did it from 148,128 cows.

In the days of the West India trade a great deal of New England cheese was sold among these islands, and still more exported to England, where it was considered better than the cheese imported from Holland.

Probably the biggest single cheese ever produced in New England was the Mammoth Cheese of Cheshire, Massachusetts, which was as big as a bass drum and weighed 1,450 pounds. It is now nearly a century and a half since Elder John Leland of Cheshire, a small agricultural town in the Berkshire Hills, persuaded the farmers of that community to contribute the milk from one day's milking for the purpose of making a colossal cheese to be presented to President Thomas Jefferson of the United States. The suggestion was received enthusiastically by the farmers, and on the appointed day, July 20, 1801, they came from miles around in every sort of conveyance, bringing their donations of milk to the place chosen for the making of the huge cheese.

As no ordinary cheese press was big enough for so stupendous an undertaking, a cider press, its sides reinforced with hoops, was used to press the cheese. Even this proved inadequate for all the curds supplied by the gracious cows of Cheshire, and three smaller cheeses were made at the same time as the big one. These extra cheeses weighed seventy pounds apiece. A whole month was spent in pressing the giant cheese, which on August 20 was carefully taken from the press and placed in a cheese house to ripen. Here it was solicitously tended for many weeks. Turning over so large a cheese without cracking it was a delicate operation, but this was done daily without mishap throughout the long ripening period.

At length it was judged that the Mammoth Cheese was ready for shipment to Washington. It was placed on a pung, and Elder John Leland and a friend conveyed it to Hudson, New York, where it was transferred to a sailing vessel and taken down the Hudson River to New York City. From here the rest of the journey to Washington was made by land, six horses with beribboned bridles drawing the wagon containing the big cheese. It reached Washington safely in good condition on December 29, 1801, and on New Year's Day, 1802, Elder Leland presented it to President Jefferson.

The ceremony took place in the East Room of the White House before a large and distinguished gathering. Wielding a huge knife, President Jefferson cut the first slice, saying as the knife sank through the cheese, "I will cause this auspicious event to be placed on the records of our nation and it will ever shine amid its glorious archives."

A generous-sized piece of the cheese was given by the president to Elder Leland to take back to the people of Cheshire, to satisfy them of its excellence; and pieces were also sent to the governors of the several states.

In September, 1940, the old wooden signboard

in Cheshire commemorating the Mammoth Cheese was superseded by a more fitting memorial dedicated by the Sons of the American Revolution. This memorial is in the form of a cider press, like the one in which the cheese was made, with a bronze plaque on the front bearing a likeness of Elder John Leland and beneath it an inscription containing the words BIG CHEESE 1754–1841.

The great cheese of Cheshire was the forerunner of a number of uncommonly large cheeses made in other communities. In 1835 the *American Magazine*, published in Boston, took notice of a number of such cheeses made by Colonel T. S. Meacham of Sandy Creek, Oswego County, New York, the largest of which weighed 1,400 pounds and was designed as a gift to President Andrew Jackson. The cheese was encircled by a belt on which was an inscription referring to Old Hickory's services to the Republic. Two others weighing 750 pounds each were intended for Martin Van Buren, Vice-President of the United States, and William L. Marcy, Governor of New York. Several others of 700 pounds each were for the Congress of the United States, the Legislature of New York, the City of Washington, and Daniel Webster. All were inscribed, the one to Webster with these words: "Liberty and union, now and forever, one and inseparable."

The editor of the *American Magazine*, after expressing the hope that the cheeses would reach the persons for whom they were intended in good order and serve to extend the fame of their industrious and generous architect, said, "The publishers of the *American Magazine* would be thankful for a cheese of half the weight of the smallest above described."

An amusing cheese story is told of William Goffe, one of the judges who condemned King Charles I, and a high officer in Cromwell's Army, who, on the restoration of Charles II to the throne, fled to New England, arriving in Boston with another Regicide, his father-in-law, General Edward Whalley, in July, 1660. While the Regicides were in Boston a fencing master erected on the Common a stage which he walked for several days, challenging and defying anyone to fight him with swords. At length Goffe, disguised in rustic dress and armed with a large cheese wrapped in a cloth for a shield and a mop besmeared with dirty puddle water for a weapon, mounted the stage. The fencing master railed at him for his impudence, asked him what business he had there, and bid him begone. But Goffe stood his ground, whereupon the gladiator made a pass at him with his sword to drive him from the platform. Goffe received the sword in the cheese, and, holding it there, drew the mop gently over the master's mouth, giving the gentleman a pair of whiskers. The expert made another thrust, and again the sword was caught and held in the cheese, while the mop was drawn gently over his eyes. The third lunge was received and held in the same way, until Goffe had rubbed the mop all over the champion's face.

Thoroughly enraged, the fencing master dropped his small sword and caught up a broadsword, at which Goffe cried, "Stop, sir! Hitherto I have only played with you, and not attempted to harm you, but if you come at me now with the broadsword, know that I will certainly kill you."

So firmly did he speak that the fencing master desisted.

"Who can you be?" he exclaimed. "You must be either Goffe, or Whalley, or the Devil, for there are no other persons who could beat me."

Three small cheeses washed up in a tangle of seaweed were the only civilized food vouchsafed to the shipwrecked crew of the "Nottingham," a Boston-bound London galley, when that vessel went on the rocks at Boon Island, Maine, the night of December 10, 1710. This tiny offshore island, which is said to have received its name because it once proved a boon to some shipwrecked mariners, lies nearly six miles to the southeast of Cape Neddick. In the bights to the north and south of the cape, which extends out about a mile from the main shore, is the summer resort of York Beach, and on Boon Island stands the tallest lighthouse on the Maine coast; but in 1710 there was no light on the rock and few persons living along the shore in the vicinity of the headland.

The "Nottingham" had been running a westerly course along the Maine coast and had hauled south for Boston when she struck Boon Island. It was a very bad night at sea. A northeasterly gale, with rain, hail, and snow, was raging, and it was as dark as the inside of a whale. A berth of a few hundred yards either way might have taken the "Nottingham" safely past Boon Island, but she drove head on into the ledges and, when she struck, all her masts went by the board. Fortunately, the foremast in falling became wedged among the rocks in such a way as to bridge the gap between ship and shore, and along it John Deane, the master, and his crew crawled to the safety of the island. But their troubles were not over when they landed.

Practically nothing was saved from the ship, which went to pieces during the night. A makeshift shelter, however, was constructed from remnants of spars and sails that were washed ashore. The mainland, in plain sight, gave them hope of deliverance, but as the days passed and no one came to their rescue their position became desperate. Several vessels were sighted, but none on board saw their signals of distress. They built a boat which, on being launched, was smashed to bits against the rocks. Two of the crew tried to reach the mainland on a raft but were never seen alive again. Incredible as it may seem, the shipwrecked crew was on the rock for twenty-four days before they were discovered and the survivors taken off. The three small cheeses did not last long, and the unhappy cook, his occupation gone, died, as did also another member of the crew. In their dire need John Deane and his men decided on a last desperate measure to save themselves. The ship's carpenter must have shed a bitter tear when he learned of the plan. For his mates had decided to eat him. He was forty-seven and plump. But he wasn't murdered, as he most conveniently died from exposure. This resort to cannibalism and the strict rationing of the carpenter's body by John Deane saved them from starving to death. But in the end it was the raft washed up on the main shore that led to a search being made for them and their rescue from Boon Island.

From Massachusetts comes a delightful tale of cheesemongering. In the olden times many ministers received a large share of their household supplies from their parishioners, and, if these were not forthcoming, did not hesitate to ask for them directly or indirectly. A Newbury minister, who in his apple piety was very fond of cheese, finding that his supply was running low, got into his sleigh one winter afternoon and drove from one house to another, expressing the wish that he might have a slice of the excellent cheese made in the house, because his wife was expecting company. It was growing dark when he turned homeward, but it was not so dark that when, in the middle of town, he accidentally overturned his sleigh, the people who went to his rescue could not see what fell out in the snow with the parson. To their amazement, no less than nine great cheeses rolled out in the roadway.

TO BE FOND OF FISH

OLD traditional street names with their antique associations have an interest and importance which new names with their ready-made associations lack. Whenever one of the old names is obliterated, a valuable historical record is destroyed. Yet, in spite of the numerous changes that have been made, most New England towns and cities have managed to retain many of their old topographical labels.

Harm! boys, harm!
A little more liquor
Will do us no harm!

Noah Webster, the great lexicographer, who was born and reared in the Connecticut Valley, wrote from personal knowledge of our river fish when he stated in his dictionary that the flesh of the shad when fresh is delicious. Epicures have always considered it a delicacy, but there was a time when shad was generally looked upon as a rather plebeian fish and was generally ignored in favor of salmon, which prior to the Civil War teemed in the river. At that time shad were so common during the spring runs that in shoal water there were actually fish jams, the Yankee farmers gathering the helplessly packed fish by the cartload for use as fertilizer on their fields. But when the salmon began to disappear from the Connecticut, people turned to shad, which rose rapidly in popular esteem. By 1860 the salmon were so far gone that shad fishing became a commercial industry.

Unfortunately, however, when this occurred the shad in turn began to decline both in numbers and in weight. Statistics of the Connecticut fisheries disclose the alarming extent of the falling-off. In 1879 the catch ran to upward of 436,000 fish, a figure which by 1922 had shrunk to 13,800, or a loss in a little over forty years of nearly ninety-seven per cent. In weight, too, the fish showed a lamentable decline. One still hears the expression used of a person, "He looks like the last run of shad," or, "As thin as a June shad," meaning he appears to be played out, not what he used to be, a wreck. Doubtless that is the way many of the shad caught today would appear by contrast if placed alongside the shad of former days. The average shad now weighs only three or four pounds, whereas formerly it weighed five or six.

Various reasons have been given for this sad decline in the numbers and weight of the Connecticut River shad. The chief causes are said to be impassable dams, overfishing, and fishing out of season. In their annual upstream pilgrimage the first dam the fish encounter is the rather low one at Enfield, near the Massachusetts line. This dam is not insurmountable, but the big dam at Holyoke is too formidable for even the most vaultingly ambitious fish to pass. In 1932 shad in considerable numbers successfully negotiated the passage of the Enfield obstruction, only to be stopped dead when they reached the Holyoke barrier. Here young men and boys, wading out below the dam, caught them with their bare hands.

In the horse and buggy age a large part of the shad catch was sold right on the riverbank, and inland folk drove long distances to the fishing places. When the fish were plentiful and cheap, a family would buy from twenty to a hundred shad to salt, in addition to those purchased to be eaten fresh. If the supply exceeded the demand at the river, the shad were loaded into wagons and peddled through the back-country towns and villages, fifteen or twenty miles from the river. Eels and alewives were also sometimes disposed of in this way, the peddlers crying them through the streets.

In Hartford, shad were at one time sold from carts or stalls in State House Square. Many a Connecticut lawmaker returned home from a session of the legislature with his saddlebags stuffed with shad. In later years, Johnny Flynn's Market, next to the stone-arched bridge on Main Street, always had the first Connecticut River shad of the season. No other marketman ever succeeded in getting ahead of Johnny Flynn. The notice of the arrival of the first shad was chalked up on a blackboard beside the doorway. It was also heralded in the newspapers, for Johnny Flynn's announcement was important local news. It meant that the long-anticipated spring phenomenon of the shad run had gotten under way.

Meanwhile, at Honiss's Oyster House—a Hartford institution still doing business after nearly a hundred years of service—shad from the Chesapeake region and the Delaware had been on the menu for some time. A local patron might concede that a Crisfield shad as served at Honiss's was delectable, but he would never admit that it was as good as a New England shad. So strong was this faith in the superior qualities of the latter that shad caught in the Connecticut River used to sell at a premium.

When I asked John Moore, the shad expert at Honiss's, how he told a buck shad from a roe shad, he said, "If there's any doubt, you squeeze the fish near the tail end of the belly. If eggs pop out, it's a roe; if milt comes, it's a buck."

He picked up a shad from its bed of ice in a barrel and demonstrated how he pressed with his thumbs to determine the sex of the fish, if it was not apparent from its size.

"Lamprey eels," he said, "suck the eggs right out of a roe shad. There'll be a red mark on the belly around the place I just showed you and not a bit of roe left. That's what eels live on."

"People as a rule prefer buck shad to roe shad, don't they?" I asked.

"It's better eating," he replied. "The flesh is firmer."

"I don't see any planked shad on the menu," I said.

"That's mostly for outings," he explained.

"You've seen them do it, haven't you? The shad is nailed to the wood, then propped up before the fire. The nails are driven through pieces of salt pork. The best fire is a birch fire."

The discovery a few years ago that the bones of a shad which are seemingly countless could be removed by an operation has increased the demand for this fish. Many people who liked shad would not eat it because they felt that contending with so many bones was more trouble than it was worth. The old school of shad eaters, however, insists on the bones, claiming that a shad cooked with the bones embedded in the flesh has a better flavor than one that has had them removed. But since at places like Honiss's you can buy shad in season either boned or unboned, it is a case of pay your money and take your choice.

Symbolic of the importance which was attached to the river fisheries in bygone days is the fact that the city of Hartford adopted a piscatorial design for its first corporate seal. In 1785, Colonel Samuel Wyllys and John Trumbull were appointed a committee to select a design for a city seal, and their recommendation was accepted. Their specifications called for the following: "Connecticut River represented by the figure of an old man with rushes seated against a rock, holding an urn with a stream flowing from it; at his feet a net, and fish peculiar to the river lying by it, with a barrel and bales; over his head an oak growing from a cleft in the rock, and round the whole these words: *Sigillum Civitatis Hartfordiensis.*" From the impressions of the seal which I have seen it is difficult to say whether "the fish peculiar to the river" are shad or salmon, or if they represent a mixed haul. In any case, the seal with the fish served the city until the present fishless device was adopted in 1852.

Fred Hale, veteran Connecticut River shad fisherman, was working in his victory garden when I found him one afternoon late in May. Mr. Hale, who lives on the green at Wethersfield, only a few hundred feet from the largest elm tree in America, is eighty-four years old. He began fishing for shad in 1879. His father was a fisherman before him. The business is a seasonal one, and when the fish stopped running Mr. Hale used to turn his hand to other things. In August he gathered skullcap along the river for a firm of manufacturing druggists, and in winter trapped muskrats. He still mends clocks and makes telescopes and other instruments, and sometimes acts as night ferryman at the Rocky Hill crossing of the Connecticut River, when he usually has an eel trap attached to the ferryboat.

"There were salmon in the river when I began fishing," he told me, "but they were getting scarce then. They stopped coming about 1890. I have known alewops to appear as early as March sixth, but the earliest shad I remember was on the sixth of April. Nine pounds is the biggest shad I ever caught, but I once got a striped bass in the river that weighed fifty-five or sixty pounds, and a sturgeon weighing one hundred and fifty. The average shad used to weigh about five pounds, and we got fifteen dollars a hundredweight for them. When the shad were running good, it was usual to get a hundred and fifty or two hundred in one haul, and you could pull your net several times a night. Shad fishing's a night job, except when the water's muddy."

"Do the shad put up much of a fight when you haul them in?" I asked.

"They are pretty lively," he said.

"When you were in the business, Mr. Hale, did you use a gill net or a hauling seine?"

"I used to fish off the old steamboat landing, and I liked to use a gill net."

"It's a big net, isn't it?"

"A gill net's about thirty-five rods long. At least, that's the length I used. A hauling seine is longer. About forty-five rods, I should say. When you put out a gill net the current carries it downstream and you drift along beside it in your boat. It's bad business when your net catches on a stump. It's an accident you hope won't happen. If it does, you have to get the location well fixed in your mind, so you can avoid the place next time. There's a lot in knowing where the snags are."

Mr. Hale invited me into his house while he looked for his fishing log, a complete record of his many years as a river fisherman. In one drawer he found a homemade wooden shuttle used in making and mending nets, which had some initials on it and the date, 1844; but the log with its valuable record of catches and prices could not be found.

"I remember when peddlers used to come from Vermont to buy alewops and shad," he said. "They brought maple sugar with them to trade for fish. The cakes were big ones. Must have weighted four or five pounds apiece."

"When is the spawning season over, Mr. Hale?"

"From the twentieth to the twenty-fifth of June," he said.

Although the bulk of the Connecticut River shad catch has always been made with nets by men like Fred Hale, shad fishing with rod and reel has recently attracted many anglers. They seem to have first turned their attention to this unusual sport in the season of 1941, when they were barred from stream fishing because of the hazardous fire conditions that existed in the woodlands and brushlands of southern New England. By requiring a special permit for this fishing, the Fisheries and Game Department was able to keep track of the number of shad caught with rod and line. The returns for the season showed that three thousand anglers caught six thousand shad, most of them in the fast water below the Enfield dam.

While Fishfry Street is apparently a unique name, there is, or was, in West Springfield a Shad Lane, extending from the common eastward to the Connecticut River. It derived its name from the vast quantities of shad formerly taken from the river at the end of the lane. It is said that one man alone with a scoop net could get as many as a thousand in a single day; but shad sold then for only two cents apiece.

Salmon were also caught at this place in large numbers. Sewall White, the old-time chronicler of West Springfield, says he remembers seeing a hundred fine specimens lying together on the shore at the fishing place of Holman Day and Tilly Merrick. Of this catch, one salmon in particular was very far from being a despicable fish; it weighed forty-two pounds. Using shad roe for bait, Sewall White himself, while standing in a fishing boat, caught and flung upon the bank in the course of a single morning eight splendid bass. Once he took a twelve-pounder from the river, but his neighbor,

Justin Ely, beat him by hooking and landing a bass weighing twenty-two pounds.

But the Shad Lane story I like best has nothing to do with fish. The lane led to the old Springfield ferry, and down it one day rode General Washington. This was during the only visit he made to New England while he was president. He rode in his private coach driven by his own colored coachman. In the lane at the time, also proceeding toward the ferry, was Jonathan Parsons, who was driving his two yoke of oxen and his horse attached to a great load of stalks. When two mounted men overtook him and ordered him to turn out for General Washington, who was on his way to the ferry, Jonathan Parsons refused, saying he had as much right to the road as the general. He probably said this not out of churlishness but because he did not believe the horsemen. In any case, General Washington's coach managed to pass him, and while waiting at the ferry, Parsons, who caught up with the equipage, heard the president say, "That man was right. He had as good a right to the road as I have."

Will shad ever return to the Connecticut River in large numbers? The question has been often asked during recent years, and most people have answered by shaking their heads and saying it was only a matter of a little time when the fish would stop their annual visits altogether. The pollution of the river and the spoiling of the spawning beds, they point out, is enough to discourage any tourist fish. But the ways of fish, like the ways of man, cannot always be accurately predicted, and suddenly in the meatless spring of 1943 the shad returned to the river in unparalleled numbers. Cliff Knight, the fish and game writer of the *Hartford Times*, reported one haul near Windsor of three thousand fish, all of which, with the exception of five hundred, were ripe roe shad. And similar reports of big hauls poured in from points up and down the river. Whether or not this large-scale renewal of acquaintance with the shad will continue, no man can say. If it does, perhaps the old glories of Fishfry Street will be revived.

TO INDULGE IN BUNDLING

WHAT is the truth about the old New England custom of bundling, which had its rise in the severe weather conditions which prevail throughout the region during part of the year? Was this antique winter sport as innocent as some have said it was, or was it, as others have alleged, a low and immoral practice? New England has long been taunted with this unpuritan custom which permitted a young courting couple to spend the night together in the same bed either fully or only partly clad. It flourished, paradoxically enough, while the shadow of Calvin was still over the land and the private life of everyone was the intimate concern of the whole community, especially of those ardent investigators into local sin—the clergy.

Yet there were clergymen who condoned bundling, and some who even approved the custom. Others actually engaged in the practice themselves. One candidate for ordination, who later became a distinguished minister, wooed a number of girls, with at least one of whom, according to an entry in his diary, he bundled *magna cum voluptate*.

The Rev. Samuel Peters, author of the *General History of Connecticut* (1781), gave bundling a clean bill of health. He said it was not only a Christian custom, but a very polite and prudent one. The modesty of Connecticut females was such, he decleared, that it would have been accounted the greatest rudeness to mention to a lady a garter or leg, yet it was thought but a piece of civility to ask her to bundle. But Mr. Peters as a social historian is unreliable. He had a rich talent for invention, one of his most notorious hoaxes being the spurious code of blue laws, which he promulgated out of whole cloth in the same work in which he discussed bundling. Yet there were people who shared his opinion that bundling was an innocent pastime, a view reflected in the following contemporary lines:

> Let coat and shift be turned adrift,
> And breeches take their flight,
> An honest man and virgin can
> Lie quiet all the night.

But when western Massachusetts became a hotbed of bundling Jonathan Edwards at Northampton raised his voice in stern warning against the custom, the consequences of which were only too evident in the number of babies born in less than the orthodox period after marriage. All over New England during the period of the Great Revival couple after couple stood up in open meeting and confessed to sexual intimacy before marriage.

In 1781, the Rev. Mr. Haven of Dedham, Massachusetts, shocked at the increase of sexual incontinence in his vicinage, attacked the growing sin in a memorable discourse in which he attributed the fault "to the custom then prevalent of females admitting young men to their beds who sought their company with intentions of marriage." The trouble was, of course, that marriage did not necessarily follow a course of bundling, and unless nature called a halt and precipitated a choice by the girl, there was danger that indulgence in the custom would lead to promiscuity.

It must be said, however, that despite the fact that bundling was done under cover in the dark, there was nothing furtive about it. Parents took the custom as a matter of course, the mother and sisters of the fortunate girl often helping to tuck the courting couple in bed together. Everything was done without self-consciousness. At the same time, the extreme temptation involved in the situation was recognized, as the girl was frequently swathed like a mummy, or her legs were tied together, or a dividing board or other object placed between the bundlers and sleigh bells attached to the bed. But love laughs at token safeguards of this kind, and whether a case turned out to be one of guilt or innocence, conquest or control, rested ultimately, as it always has, with the young people themselves.

It has been claimed that one of the economic elements centering in the custom was the practical importance to a couple of knowing in advance of marriage whether or not they could have children to aid them in the struggle of life. It is true that bundling was a country custom; children were valuable assets in the agricultural life of the time, and apparently no special stigma attached to anyone if a baby was born seven months after marriage; but to say that young people married to solve the labor problem is to rule out romantic love and place matrimony on a rather sordid plane. The upper strata of New England town society, which did not practice bundling, admittedly took a decidedly mercenary view of marriage, as is shown by all the bickering and litigation there was over marriage settlements, but even among these people marriages were not contracted exclusively on a basis of mutual gain in worldly goods.

The conditions which favored bundling among rustic New Englanders were poorness of communications and the necessity of conserving heat and light. A country youth who had worked hard from sunrise to sunset all the week would set out on Saturday night to see his best girl. Habitations were widely spaced in those days, and the young man might have to walk from six to a dozen miles to reach the girl's house. The week end from sundown Saturday to sundown Sunday was practically the only time he had for courting. Families were large and houses small, with all beds occupied, and while the young couple could have sat up all night, this would have necessitated the expenditure of light and fuel which were too precious to be wasted in this way. So instead of turning the young man out in the cold, he and the girl enjoyed each other's company in comfort by lying snugly together under the quilts in her feather bed.

Although this week-end country custom was extremely popular throughout New England, it neither originated here nor was it confined exclusively to New England. New Englanders blamed it on the Dutch, and the Dutch on the New Englanders. An amusing passage in Washington Irving's *Knickerbocker's History of New York*, ascribes bundling to the inventive genius of the Connecticut Yankees, who, it is said, practiced it to keep up a harmony of interests and to promote the population.

"They multiplied to a degree," Irving wrote, "which would be incredible to any man unacquainted with the marvelous fecundity of this young country. This amazing increase may, indeed, be partly ascribed to a singular custom prevalent among them, commonly known by the name of *bundling*—a superstitious rite observed by the young people of both sexes, with which they usually terminate their festivities, and which was kept up with religious strictness by the more bigoted and vulgar of the community.

"This ceremony was likewise, in those primitive times, considered as an indispensable preliminary to matrimony; their courtships commencing where ours usually finish, by which means they acquired that intimate acquaintance with each other before marriage, which has been pronounced by philosophers the sure basis of a happy union. Thus early did this cunning and ingenious people display a shrewdness at making a bargain, which has ever since distinguished them, and a strict adherence to the good old vulgar maxim about 'buying a pig in a poke.'

"To this sagacious custom, therefore, do I chiefly attribute the unparalleled increase of the Yanokie or Yankee tribe; for it is a certain fact, well authenticated by court records and parish registers, that wherever the practice of bundling prevailed, there was an amazing number of sturdy brats annually born unto the state, without the licence of the law or the benefit of clergy. Neither did the irregularity of their birth operate in the least to their disparagement. On the contrary, they grew up a long-sided, raw-boned race of whoreson whalers, wood cutters, fishermen and peddlers; and strapping corn-fed wenches, who by their united efforts tended marvelously toward populating those notable tracts of country called Nantucket, Piscataway and Cape Cod."

This humorous passage by Washington Irving contains more fiction than fact. For the truth of the matter seems to be that the custom of bundling has arisen independently in isolated sections of different countries, and how New England caught it, found it, or came by it is a baffling question.

No less a person than Charles Francis Adams read a paper on bundling before the Massachusetts Historical Society in which he said, "The most singular, and to me unaccountable, fact connected with the custom of bundling is that though it unquestionably prevailed—and prevailed long, generally, and from an early period—in New England, no trace has been reported of it in any localities of England itself, the mother country. There are well-authenticated records of its prevalence in parts at least of Ireland, Wales, Scotland, and Holland; but it could hardly have found its way as a custom from any of those countries to New England. I well remember hearing the late Dr. John G. Palfrey remark—and the remark will, I think, very probably be found in some note to the text of his *History of New England*—that down to the beginning of the present century, or about the year 1825, there was a purer strain of English blood to be found in the inhabitants of Cape Cod than could be found in any county of England. The original settlers of that region were exclusively English, and for the first two centuries after the settlement there was absolutely no foreign admixture. Yet nowhere in New England does the custom of bundling seem to have prevailed more generally than on Cape Cod; and according to Dr. Stiles it was on Cape Cod that the practice held out the longest against the advance of more refined manners."

The general prevalence of bundling in rural New England made Mr. Adams wonder whether traces of it could be found in the traditions and records of any of our large towns. Although the sermon of Mr. Haven of Dedham showed that it was commonly practiced within a radius of ten miles of Boston, Mr. Adams greatly doubted whether it ever obtained in Boston itself. "Nevertheless," he said, "an examination of the church records of Boston, Salem, and more especially of Plymouth, would be interesting, with a view to ascertaining whether the spirit of sexual incontinence prevailed during the last century in the large towns of New England to the same extent to which it unquestionably prevailed in the rural districts. My own belief is that it did so prevail, though the practice of bundling was not in use; if I am correct in this assumption, it would follow that the evil was a general one, and that bundling was merely the custom through which it found vent. In such case the cause of the evil would have to be looked for in some other direction. It would then, paradoxically as such a statement may at first appear, probably be found in the superior general morality of the community and the strict oversight of a public opinion which, except in Boston—a large commercial place, where there was always a considerable floating population of sailors and others—prevented the recognized existence of any class of professional prostitutes. On the one hand, a certain form of incontinence was not associated either in the male or female mind with the presence of a degraded class, while, on the other hand, the natural appetites were to a certain extent gratified. It was in their attempt to wholly ignore these natural appetites that Jonathan Edwards and the clergy of the last century fell into their error."

With this statement by the distinguished Massachusetts historian we may well leave the old New England custom of bundling.

TO TALK ABOUT THE WEATHER

MARK TWAIN did not exaggerate greatly when he said New England had no climate—only weather. There was a sumptuous variety about this weather, he declared, that compelled the stranger's admiration and regret. The only certain thing about it was that you could be sure there would be plenty of it. Every year, he went on to say, New Englanders killed a lot of poets for writing about the beautiful spring. These poets were mostly visiting versifiers who didn't know what they were talking about.

The New England poets themselves have, of course, always handled the weather extremely well. Some of the best known American poetry is the work of these men writing about local meteorological conditions. "What is so rare as a day in June?" asked Lowell, who was also the author of the familiar poem, "The First Snowfall," which opens with the lines:

> The snow had begun in the gloaming,
> And busily all the night
> Had been heaping field and highway
> With a silence deep and white.

Probably an even better known winter piece is Whittier's cheerful "Snowbound," with its atmosphere of comfortable isolation and snug security. But the New England poets could take the bitter with the sweet, as witness Bryant's "Death of the Flowers," which begins with the deathless lines:

> The melancholy days are come,
> The saddest of the year.

And fairly dripping with gloom are these words of Longfellow:

> The day is cold and dark and dreary,
> It rains and the wind is never weary.

Longfellow knew his omens. A halo round the sun or moon does presage rain, and his mariner in "The Wreck of the Hesperus" was right in taking it as a bad sign that

> "Last night the moon had a golden ring,
> And tonight no moon I see."

In the Great Hurricane of 1815 Oliver Wendell Holmes lost his Sunday pants but, as one would expect, made light of his loss. He was a boy of seven at the time, and the pants, which were hanging on the line, were whisked away by the wind. He saw them sailing through the air, but too late to retrieve them, and they were never found. When he grew to manhood he wrote some amusing verses lamenting their disappearance.

> They were my darlings and my pride,
> My boyhood's only riches—
> "Farewell, farewell," I faintly cried—
> "My breeches! O my breeches!"

Even Mark Twain admitted there was one feature of New England weather that produced an effect of surpassing beauty and brilliance. This occurred when the rain froze on the trees during a winter night, coating them with ice down to the tiniest twig, and then, the weather having cleared, the morning sun set them to flashing and sparkling like crystal fountains.

Incidentally, it was not Mark Twain, but his Hartford neighbor, Charles Dudley Warner, who made the classic remark, "Everybody talks about the weather, but nobody does anything about it."

Another agreeable aspect of the New England year is the period of mild weather in October called Indian summer, when the air is soft and balmy and usually filled with a slight haze, like purple smoke. The ideal temperature suggests spring, yet Indian summer is not like spring. For one thing, it smells differently. Spring has a fresh, new, green smell, whereas the smell of Indian summer is like the mature and nutty bouquet of some tawny old wine. The Indians ascribed the cause of this delightful season to the southwest wind blowing directly from the court of their great and benevolent god, Cautantowit, or southwestern god, who sent them whatever blessings they enjoyed and to whom their fathers went when they died.

How the season got its name nobody knows. Professor Kittredge of Harvard says there is no evidence that it was used in early colonial times or that the whites derived it from the Indians. The earliest recorded mention of Indian summer is 1794. Various guesses have been made as to the origin of the term. There is, of course, nothing more fickle than the weather in Indian summer—which as a season may last for only two or three days or extend over a period of two or three weeks—and it has been suggested that the name alludes to the proverbial instability, deceitfulness, and treachery of the Indians. But the explanation I like best is that of a person I know who as a child thought Indian summer was called by that name because the trees which are then decked in the ceremonial colors of autumn were dressed like Indians.

Days of fasting and prayer were customarily observed in New England during periods of afflicting weather, especially droughts, of which there were many. If relief came before the designated fast day arrived, it was changed to one of thanksgiving. People then, of course, saw the hand of God in more things than they do today. According to Alice Morse Earle, one New England minister during a long spell of dryness petitioned for rain in these words:

"O Lord, Thou knowest we do not want Thee to send us a rain which shall pour down in fury and swell our streams and carry away our haycocks, fences, and bridges; but, Lord, we want it to come drizzle-drozzle, drizzle-drozzle for about a week. Amen."

The New England churches themselves have through the years often been grievously injured by the action of the elements. In the Great Hurricane which scourged New England in September, 1938, hundreds of churches were severely damaged, many losing their steeples, while others were completely wrecked. This tropical storm, which blew in from off the Bahamas toward Florida, before reaching the mainland turned northward and, roaring up the coast, smote New England, cost six hundred lives, millions of trees, and staggering losses in buildings, barns, cottages, and other species of property. Few churches in the path of the storm escaped damage.

The Rev. Warren S. Archibald of the Second Congregational Church of Hartford, Connecticut, spent the night of the hurricane on the roof of his church. He heard that the church had been damaged and at the earliest possible moment went to investigate. The church is a large one, and it was a horrifying sight, he said, to see the vast tin roof on the entire south side stripped off and hanging in shreds from the eaves like wallpaper. The rain had already damaged the ceiling of the church. He got hold of a member of the church committee and also a builder, who worked all night with his men putting on a temporary roof of tar paper. For a while after the hurricane had passed, considerable apprehension was felt, as it was believed to be only half over. They thought that they were in the dead center of the storm and would have to go through the other half. This, however, proved not to be the case, and the night turned out to be a fine one—clear, starry, and windless.

'Tis an ill wind that blows no good, and one church in a small Massachusetts town was actually improved by this same tempest. There were two rich families in the town, one of which had given the church its steeple, a lovely spire in perfect keeping with the general architecture of the building. But the other rich family, not to be outdone, spoiled it all by sticking Byzantine pinnacles all over the place. The hurricane did not harm the steeple, but it tore off the Byzantine ornaments, and thus was the church purified and restored by the storm.

But probably the most extraordinary adventure ever to befall a New England church occurred many years before this, during the spring freshet of

1823, when the Methodist meetinghouse at Norwich, Connecticut, was swept down the Thames River into Long Island Sound, narrowly missing a schooner in New London Harbor as it passed out to sea. A torrential downpour lasting twenty-four hours caused a rapid rise in the river which carried away the church before it could be anchored. It had been decorated with evergreens for some special occasion and was still adorned with these when it set sail on its unusual voyage. Moving like a stately ship, rising and falling with the waves as it moved along with the current, it remained upright for a considerable distance, its stoutly pegged frame proving surprisingly seaworthy.

All sorts of wild stories grew out of the incident, one newspaper reporting that the minister and his flock were in the church at the time and could be heard singing lustily as they passed New London; while another paper said that the meetinghouse had gone ashore on one of the islands in the Sound, where, according to a notice which had been given, future services would be held.

The schooner which the drifting church nearly ran down in New London Harbor was the "Fame" from Charleston, South Carolina, bound for Bridgeport, Connecticut. The crew said that when the meetinghouse sailed proudly past them in the night as they lay at anchor it was brightly lighted. The

Connecticut poet, John G. C. Brainard, wrote a ballad about the narrow escape of the Charleston vessel beset by the Yankee meetinghouse, but it is not a very good ballad, though Brainard was a genuine poet.

It is a pity that no poet seems to have written about Hosea Keach's ride, which, though not so well-known an episode of New England history as Paul Revere's ride, was in some ways more remarkable. Hosea was the last of the toll takers at the old covered wooden bridge which spanned the Connecticut River between Enfield and Suffield, Connecticut. When at the beginning of the century it was swept away by a freshet, Hosea went with it, gallantly riding the ancient arklike structure on the raging ice-strewn flood, until he was rescued in a climax as thrilling as that of any melodrama of the horse and buggy days.

During the last years of its existence business at the bridge became so bad that the income from tolls was insufficient to pay the keeper and make the necessary repairs. Always the keeper had been permitted to carry on his own trade at the bridge. One was a weaver who had in the tollhouse a carpet loom on which he wove rugs for the farmers' wives from materials which they brought him. Another was a cigar maker. Still another was a cobbler. But when more convenient crossings above and below the old bridge took all the carriage trade, the tollkeeper's private business suffered with the decline of the public bridge business. It was a relief to the owner of the bridge, when, about three years before its destruction, it was, for reasons of public safety, ordered closed to traffic. A few pedestrians and cyclists made breaches in the barriers and still used it, while Hosea Keach continued to live in the tollkeeper's house. Here he could keep an eye on the bridge and at the same time serve the New York, New Haven, and Hartford Railroad as agent at the Enfield Bridge Station near the tollhouse.

Two and a half miles downstream, the main line of the New Haven Railroad crosses the Connecticut River at Windsor Locks. If the heavily-timbered Enfield Bridge should be washed away, the railroad bridge might be seriously endangered, so Hosea Keach was instructed to inspect the old bridge regularly and report on its condition. It was common knowledge that the seventy-year-old structure was pretty shaky.

During the high water of February, 1900, Hosea became unusually vigilant. On the afternoon of the fifteenth, shortly before the two-thirty southbound train from Springfield was due, he went out on the bridge to look at the central span, so he could report to the conductor of the train. He had gone only part way when he heard a great tearing and rending of timbers and, realizing that the bridge was going, turned and ran for his life. He had almost reached the end of the bridge when the floor suddenly buckled and heaved upward, and, the next thing Hosea knew, he was perched among the cobwebs on one of the crosspieces in the easterly gable of the bridge.

"The span shut up like a jackknife," he said afterward. "Timbers of the bridge rose before me in the air. I thought they were going to fall on me."

For a time Hosea's mind seems to have been a blank, but when he came to himself he realized that the bridge was moving with the current, as the floor had dropped out and the surging waters of the river were slipping past below him; but he could not see outside to get his bearings. Trapped in the dim interior of the bridge, he tried unsuccessfully to beat out some of the roof and gable boards with his bare hands. Then by the flickering light that came through the cracks in the old structure he discovered a loose piece of timber with which he managed to dislodge the signboard that read: WALK YOUR HORSES ACROSS THIS BRIDGE. By enlarging this hole he was at length able to crawl out to the roof of the wreck. The river above the railroad bridge is divided into two channels by Terry Island. When

Hosea got his bearings he found that he and his odd craft were heading down the easterly side of the island. He began to yell for help.

Meanwhile, the train from Springfield had reached the Enfield Bridge Station, and since Hosea was not on hand to meet it, the crew looked at the space where the covered bridge had been with a wild surmise and beat the wreckage down to the lower bridge, where men with ropes were posted to watch for Hosea.

J. Warren Johnson was in his law office in Windsor Locks that afternoon, writing a letter to the owner of the bridge and the bridge franchise, William D. Marsh of Chicago, telling him that one of the old piers was very weak indeed, when someone in the office exclaimed, "Why, what's this coming down the river?" Mr. Johnson looked out the window and saw a large section of his client's property drifting downstream. He didn't stop to write, he telegraphed.

It was shortly after three o'clock that the men at the railroad bridge sighted the span of the covered bridge with the toll taker astride it, bearing down on them. A rope with a loop in the end was let down near the place where Hosea was expected to pass. As he came within hailing distance, they shouted to him.

"Get into the loop!" they cried.

And as the old hulk passed safely under the railroad bridge, Hosea got into the loop and was drawn to safety. He didn't suffer a scratch, but he did get his pants wet.

Freshets were not the sole cause of the loss of the old covered bridges. High winds as well as high water sometimes wrecked them. This was the case with the long covered bridge which spanned the Connecticut River between Northampton and Hadley, Massachusetts. On June 14, 1876, a suddenly rising wind which speedily developed hurricane force dislodged the old wooden structure from its stone piers anchored in the bed of the stream and landed the bridge in the river.

"Eleven persons and seven teams of horses were on the bridge at the time," writes N. Seelye Hitchcock of Easthampton, who for many years was county commissioner of Hampshire County where the bridge was located. "All were precipitated into the stream. The water in the river at that time was very low, and only one person, a very young child, was drowned. Mrs. Catherine Sullivan of Hadley, however, was killed by falling timbers, and Sheriff Enos Cook, also of Hadley, was rather badly hurt by the same means.

"Charles Cook of Hadley took refuge from the wind by entering one end of the bridge accompanied by his young son. When it became apparent from the creaking that the bridge was about to collapse, they fled, and the boy was blown up into a nearby tree. Later, during the rescue work after the wind had subsided, young Cook was rescued from the tree unharmed."

The size of the old wooden affair blown into the river may be gauged by the iron one that replaced it in 1877. It measured approximately eighteen hundred feet in length. This piece of ironmongery after many vicissitudes was replaced by the present steel and concrete structure—the Calvin Coolidge Memorial Bridge—erected after the flood of 1936.

The worst flood ever to devastate New England was that of March, 1936, when all the rivers along the Atlantic seaboard from Maine to Virginia went on a rampage, inundating cities, isolating towns, and sweeping away whole villages. Many of the mill towns of New England lie dangerously close to the water line of the rivers beside which they are situated, and these places suffered appallingly. Even where every allowance had been made for high water, the damage was heavy, as the flood rose to unprecedented heights. This was true not only of the mill towns but of all riverside places. The plant of the Hartford Electric Light Company on the bank of the Connecticut River at Hartford, for example, was built with what was thought to be an ample margin of safety above the highest high water mark on record, but this was not enough, and to add to the general terror of the flood the Connecticut capital was plunged into darkness. Everywhere families clinging to the ridgepoles of their houses had to be rescued, while others reached safety by using improvised rafts. The two most sinister features of the visitation were the awful silence imposed on the stricken areas and the abominable smell of the dirty flood water.

What was the cause of this extraordinary deluge? According to the weathermen, it was the result of a freakish coincidence. A storm blowing northeastward out of Texas left a trail of heavy snow in Tennessee and North Carolina, but over the eastern watersheds it became trapped between a flow of warm, moist air from the Gulf and the Atlantic and a cold front knifing its way southward from Canada. And the rain came tumbling down. It mingled with the rapidly melting snow which still lay deep upon the ranges, and, since the ground was frozen, the runoff developed at a terrific rate. Down from the hills of New England poured the mightiest flood in the history of the region. For days after the flood receded, the rhythmic throb of pumping engines could be heard freeing buildings from water, and it took months to clear up the debris and repair the damage done.

Since then public works have been completed which provide a certain measure of protection against floods, particularly along New England's greatest river, the Connecticut. So it is not likely that we shall be so badly swamped again.

One would suppose that New England with its ups and downs of weather, its sudden and disconcerting extremes of temperature, and the outrageous habit which the seasons have of unexpectedly borrowing days from each other, would be a discouraging and baffling place for weather prophets to work. Yet from time immemorial New England has abounded in these experts, and the people have shown an almost childlike faith in the wisdom of their weathermen.

Long before the days of the Weather Bureau great confidence was placed in the predictions of the almanac makers, who foretold the weather a twelvemonth in advance. The almanacs enjoyed large circulations, and doubtless the mistakes which the old prognosticators made were, like the mistakes of politicians, soon forgotten. But people did not hesitate to complain if the prophecies proved false or the prophets failed to give notice of some unusual visitation of nature. There is a charming credulity in the complaint of the *Newport Mercury* of October 30, 1759. "We hear several vessels have been cast away in the late storm at different places. We are surprised Dr. Ames should neglect inserting this storm in his almanac, which might have prevented the fate which attended those unfortunate mariners."

On the whole, New Englanders have had good reason to rely upon the predictions of their unofficial prophets. For many of these observers, working without maps or scientific data, have developed an uncanny instinct for correctly forecasting the weather in their localities. This is particularly true in the fishing villages along the coast, where the people are engaged in the old struggle with the sea. A typical sight in one of these little ports is the fisherman at evening strolling down to the harborside to make his observations. With pipe in mouth and hands in pockets, he calmly scans the sea and sky, notes the direction of the wind, gets the general feeling of the atmosphere, and, having done this, he is able to foretell the weather for the next twenty-four hours or so with amazing accuracy. But the radio, which penetrates everywhere with its scientific predictions, is rapidly displacing the old-fashioned prophet with his keenly developed weather sense, and weather forecasting as practiced unofficially throughout New England may become a lost art.

There is, however, much sound weather lore current among New Englanders in the form of old sayings, such as "Open and shet—bound to be wet." But the most familiar and reliable of these antique saws are older than New England itself.

Fifty years ago it was a stock joke to speak of "six weeks sledding in March," and the story behind the phrase goes back perhaps another half century. It seems there was a family in Maine named Weeks which included six small Weekses. One March day one of the village wits saw the six out sledding and that evening at the general store whetted the inquisitiveness of the idlers by drawling, "Wal, I've lived to see six weeks sleddin' in March, so I reckon I know a thing or two about winters."

Phineas T. Barnum, the amiable Yankee mountebank, has told how in his native town of Bethel, Connecticut, the postrider used to clatter through the village once a week with the newspapers, crying, "News, news! The Lord reigns!" One day, when passing the schoolhouse during a snowstorm, he was heard to cry, "News, news! The Lord reigns —and also snows a little!"

The splendid lack of artistic restraint in New England weather, particularly its extremely variable character, has often caused adverse comment, but there is reason to believe that its very vagaries are one of New England's greatest assets. For the investigations of Professor Ellsworth Huntington of Yale University have shown that civilization reaches its highest levels in just those regions where, customarily, the weather is most changeable.

TO BEAT THE DRUM

NEBUCHADNEZZAR'S orchestra included the cornet, flute, harp, sackbut, psaltery, and dulcimer, but according to the Rev. Samuel A. Peters, who invented and published the imaginary blue laws of Connecticut, only half that number of instruments were in use by the colonists, as they were forbidden to play on any instruments of music "except the drum, trumpet, and jew's-harp." Of these unoutlawed instruments the drum was by far the most important. For a century or more after the first landings it was customarily used by our forefathers for religious, military, and civilian purposes.

Nathaniel Hawthorne thought it would have been by no means surprising if our pious ancestors, when they came to New England, had rejected the use of bells, refusing to be thus summoned to public worship because the same mode was practiced in the churches and high cathedrals of the ancient faith. But through necessity it was the beat of a drum, not the ringing of a bell, which at first called them on the Sabbath and lecture days.

This use of a martial instrument for church purposes was not so inappropriate as may appear at first sight. Life in those days was quasi-military in character. Every man capable of bearing arms had to be ready to stand to at a moment's notice. Training days, when there was an inspection of arms and a drill, were held at regular intervals. Every settlement of any consequence had its garrison houses, and for long periods a constant vigil had to be maintained to guard against the possibility of a surprise attack by Indians. The men went armed to meeting. One minister religiously carried his gun into the pulpit, where he stood ready to shoot the first hostile savage who poked his head through the doorway. After the sermon, the men, as a precautionary measure, always left the meetinghouse before the women and children, and in some communities this custom was observed long after the men ceased to go armed or there was any danger of attack.

The post of drummer in early New England was a paid position, and the expense was borne by the town. The drummer often provided his own instrument, but sometimes the town furnished the drum. Norwalk, Connecticut, not only supplied its drummer with a strong, new drum, but also with flax for the braces, and paid him fourteen shillings a year for his services. In 1735 the town of Windsor, Connecticut, granted John Allen the sum of twelve shillings and a sixpence for beating the drum on the Sabbath. There was a walk atop the Windsor meetinghouse built especially for the use of the drummer. It was probably not unlike the captains' walks which one sees today on the rooftops of old Nantucket houses. In New Haven one Robert Basset was hired to beat his drum "twice upon Lordes Dayes and Lecture Dayes upon the meeting house that soe those who live farr off may heare the more distinkly." Farmington bought a bell in 1731, but prior to that the people were summoned to meeting by the beating of a drum, at a cost to the town of thirty shillings a year. This was about the highest sum any drummer was paid.

The original Farmington drum, minus the hoops and heads and braces, which was presented to the Connecticut Historical Society in 1842, is among the colonial relics on exhibition in the society's rooms. It is a large drum, the shell having a depth of nineteen and a half inches and the head a diameter of twenty-one inches. Around the air hole in the side is an escutcheon and the initials L. D. worked out in small, brass-headed nails. The sound of this drum must have carried far when it was beaten with purpose and decision.

Although drums were generally used before bells became common, they were not employed everywhere. Blowing a horn, trumpet, or conch shell was preferred by some towns, and the blowers were paid as well as the beaters. At Haverhill, Massachusetts, the horn blower received from each family a pound of pork a year. And the town was proud that could boast of having both a trumpeter and a drummer.

Important as was the Sunday work of the drummer, the Sabbath was not so much of a red-letter day for him as was training day. Nothing delighted the people more at one of these field events than a contest between rival drummers. It usually came at the end of the day's exercises, while the people were still assembled on the common or green. This

said, knew their business, struck up with all the art and life of which they were masters. 'Silence, silence!' yelled the colonel, which was answered by Wadsworth's, 'Drum, drum!' Turning to his excellency, Wadsworth then said, 'If I am interrupted again I will make the sun shine through you in a moment.' So earnestly and forcefully did he say this that no further attempt was made to read or enlist men."

In Pease and Niles *Gazetteer of Connecticut and Rhode Island* (1819) there is a description of the famous Drum Rock of Rhode Island which the Indians used for purposes of communication. The rock is one of those curious natural phenomena, a tipping rock, so delicately balanced that very slight pressure starts it rocking. There are many such rocks scattered about the earth, but this one formerly differed from most in that when set in motion it made a drumming sound.

"Within a mile from the village of Apponaug," say the gazetteerists, "may be seen a huge rock, so completely balanced upon another, and its equilibrium so exact, that a boy fourteen years of age may set it in such motion that the contact or collision caused thereby, produces a sound somewhat like that of a drum, but more sonorous, which in a still evening may be heard a distance of six or eight miles. Hence, from time immemorial, it has gone by the name of the Drum Rock. From the ponderous weight of that part which is thus nicely balanced, it is generally believed, that no other than the hand of nature ever could have done it. Yet some are inclined to believe, that it was thus placed by the herculean labor of some tribe of the natives. There remains no doubt, but that this was a place of their resort or encampment; and that the Drum Rock served them either to give an alarm in case of danger, or to call the tribe together from their daily avocations. This rock is considered a great curiosity, excites much attention, and consequently is at the present day a place of much resort, particularly in the pleasant season of the year."

Another rock, a huge granite boulder, on the shore of Penobscot Bay at Castine, Maine, is memorable for having sheltered an American drummer boy during the ill-starred amphibious operations against that town when the British held it during the Revolution. The boy behind the rock, which is called after him Trask's Rock, played his instrument as his comrades stormed up the heights to take the British positions. Some versions of the story have it that young Trask was a fifer, not a drummer, but many generations of Castine children have heard the ghost of the boy beating his drum.

Timothy Dwight, who was chaplain to General Putnam's regiment in the Revolution and after-

ers, as is evident from the specimens of their handiwork which have survived, but a day spent in Bloomfield yielded little information about them or their shop. The house where they lived, a clapboard farmhouse with a central chimney which was built about 1805, is still standing on Brown Street, but the drum shop is gone. It stood to the north of the house from which it was separated by a driveway. It is described by those who remember it as a single-story building measuring perhaps fifteen by thirty feet. It was not torn down until the nineties, but no one can recall the time when drums were made there, and apparently none was produced after the death of Eli Brown in 1855, unless his brother survived him and carried on the business. I have seen it stated that Eli Brown made drums during the Revolution, but as it says on the brownstone monument over his grave in the hill cemetery that he was seventy-four when he died in 1855, this could not be true. His granddaughter, Mrs. Lillian Cairns, who lived in the old house until 1892, informed me that her father, Eli Brown, Jr., who died in 1889, was not a drum maker, though he may have occasionally repaired a drum. She did not think that Benjamin Brown, Jr., was her grandfather's brother, though she did not know the name of the brother who was associated with the elder Eli in the drum business. There were a lot of Browns in Bloomfield, and the point can perhaps be cleared up only by a search of the records.

The oldest and largest toy drum factory in the world is situated in Granville, Massachusetts, an aloof hilltop town in the western part of the state, twelve miles from the nearest railroad at Westfield. Drums have been made there for almost a century, and hundreds of thousands of them are produced annually. The industry was started in 1854, when Silas Noble and James Cooley began making drums in the kitchen of the latter's home. They made or had prepared locally all the parts for their drums, including the calfskins and sheepskins for the heads, and the leather "ears" for the braces. Few drums were sold at first, but presently several dozen were disposed of, and in a year or two the partners had to look for roomier quarters in which to carry on their business. Water power aided them in their new situation, but it was the Civil War that put the infant industry on its feet. Many military drums were made by Noble and Cooley, and most of the Massachusetts regiments were equipped by them.

In 1860 they produced one of the costliest drums ever made. It was manufactured from rails split by Abraham Lincoln, and was used in the presidential campaign of that year. The hooks were of solid silver, and the cord was of red, white, and blue silk.

Later, several years after the war, they made what was claimed to have been the world's largest civilized drum. A pair of horses could be driven through it. It was an eight-footer, and many fairs and cattle shows were visited before prize animals with hides large enough for the heads could be found. The mammoth drum was used by D. C. Hall of the famous Boston Brass Band at the Peace Jubilee in Boston in 1872, during the visit of President Grant.

Although today the Granville drums are made mainly of metal, formerly they were principally of wood, mostly chestnut, basswood, and beech, while many of the better drums were made of birch and maple. Birch is still used for drumsticks. The firm owns wood lots around Granville, whence in the past came the bulk of the material used in their drums.

First and last Noble and Cooley—the original name is still retained and Cooley's descendants carry on the business—have made about a thousand different styles of drums, ranging in size from tiny ones with paper heads measuring only six and a half inches in diameter to twenty-two-inch bass drums. Since they are designed for the toy trade, they are brightly decorated, with the colored shells turned out like postage stamps by a machine designed and developed in the drum shop. The most popular pictures on the heads of the bass drums are the Spirit of '76, Custer's Last Stand, and Robinson Crusoe. Tambourines, jazz sets, and banjo-ukes are also made here, and at one time many zithers were produced. Toy drums are sold by the dozen, but the business is largely seasonal, and in mid-December, when the Christmas demand slackens, the drum shop is closed for a spell.

Millions of drums have been made by this old firm, and if when very young you had a drum, the chances are it came from the quiet old New England town of Granville.

One of the most famous drum corps in New England was the Moodus Drum Corps of Moodus, Connecticut, in the lower valley of the Connecticut River. The Indian name for Moodus was Machimoodus, meaning place of noises, but the sounds the aboriginals had in mind when they conferred the name were not those made by the crack Moodus Drum Corps. They were thinking of the mysterious and awful rumblings of the earth, for which the place was notorious. But no less wonderful were the sounds produced by the Moodus drummers. Drumming as practiced in Moodus was a fine art, and every member of the corps was an artist. They used the old-fashioned, deep, Revolutionary style drums, heirlooms in many cases, some from the drum shop of the Brown brothers in Bloomfield, with which they produced a volume of sound that rocked the buildings along their line of march. It was, indeed, the boast of the corps that they knocked the crockery off the shelves of the houses they passed. When they really wanted to put on the pressure, they used their drumsticks in reverse. No parade anywhere in Connecticut was thought to be worth a bag of peanuts unless the deep-drum Continental boys from down the river—some were white-haired men—were in the line. Nor did anyone ever have to be told when the famous corps was approaching. There was no mistaking the deep, magnificent throb and roll of those drums and the shrilling of the Moodus fifes. It was like nothing heard before or since.

Once when the Moodus drummers came to Hartford to escort the newly elected governor to the state capital for his inauguration, they were the cause of a fiasco which it is a wonder did not prove fatal for some of the participants in the inaugural parade. While the governor and his staff were lunching at the Hartford Club, which then occupied the fine old brick Wadsworth mansion in Prospect Street, the military formed in the street outside. The escort included the New Haven Troop of Governor's Horse Guards, which had come to

Hartford by train and was mounted on local livery-stable chargers. In their dragoon uniforms the New Haven boys made a brave showing as they lined up in the street. It would perhaps be unfair to say that they were flown with insolence and wine, but it would at least probably be true to state that none was feeling despondent when the governor, top-hatted and spatted, emerged from the club with his staff, to enter the open hacks for the drive to the capital.

As the governor descended the stone steps from the pillared portico of the club, the Moodus Drum Corps suddenly struck up "Old Dan Tucker." The crash and roar of the drums coming without warning so startled the horses of the New Haven Guards that they stampeded, and the whole troop was put to flight. It was like the charge of the Light Brigade. The street was littered with dismounted troopers and their impediments, while riderless horses tore madly through the town. Yet the governor was successfully inaugurated, and by evening most of the victims had recovered sufficiently to attend the governor's ball.

The following morning the *Hartford Courant* suggested that the next time the New Haven Horse Guards came to Hartford for escort duty with the governor they should use horses and buggies, but this never became a custom.

TO REACH A RIPE OLD AGE

It is an old custom for New Englanders to live to be as old as the hills. Although longevity may not always be an amiable quality, it is usually an impressive one, and the interest which our forefathers took in centenarians is attested by the numerous accounts of such persons. Local historians never fail to mention them, and old newspapers seem to have been as fond of reporting longevities as are the newspapers of today. A man can apparently shun publicity successfully all his life, but if he lives to be a hundred, he is certain to be tracked down and dragged into the limelight.

How old the oldest inhabitant of New England was when he died, it is difficult to say for sure. Probably no one equaled the record of that "olde, olde, very olde man," Old Parr, who in the seventeenth century was the wonder of Old England and the talk of New England. This Shropshire lad lived to be one hundred and fifty-two; he was born in 1483 and died in 1635. But some impressive scores were run up in this country, and those who made them were doubtless proud to achieve great age.

Yet there was an old woman of Portsmouth, New Hampshire, who did not rejoice in being overlooked by death. She was afraid it had forgotten her altogether. When she was one hundred and two some people visited her, and while they were with her a bell was heard to toll for a funeral. The old lady burst into tears. "When will the bell toll for me?" she cried. "It seems that the bell will never toll for me. I am afraid that I shall never die."

Sympathy must be felt for this centenarian, and also for the elderly creature whom Charles Dickens met at Hartford during the course of his first American journey in 1842. While in the Connecticut capital, Dickens visited the Retreat for the Insane, which is still an important institution for the treatment of mental cases, though it now goes under another name. A few years ago it was rechristened the Neuro-Psychiatric Institute and Hospital and, still more recently, the Institute for Living.

"I very much questioned within myself, as I walked through the Insane Asylum," says Dickens in his *American Notes*, "whether I should have known the attendants from the patients, but for the few words which passed between the former, and the Doctor, with reference to the persons under their charge. Of course I limit this remark merely to their looks; for the conversation of the mad people was mad enough.

"There was one little prim old lady, of very smiling and good-humored appearance, who came sidling up to me from the end of a long passage, and with a curtsey of inexpressible condescension, propounded this unaccountable inquiry:

" 'Does Pontefract still flourish, Sir, upon the soil of England?'

" 'He does, ma'am,' I replied.

" 'When you last saw him, Sir, he was—'

" 'Well, ma'am,' said I, 'extremely well. He begged me to present his compliments. I never saw him looking better.'

"At this, the old lady was very much delighted.

After glancing at me for a moment, as if to be quite sure that I was serious in my respectful air, she sidled back some paces; sidled forward again; made a sudden skip (at which I precipitately retreated a step or two); and said:

" '*I* am an antediluvian, Sir.'

"I thought the best thing to say was, that I had suspected as much from the first. Therefore I said so.

" 'It is an extremely proud and pleasant thing, Sir, to be an antediluvian,' said the old lady.

" 'I should think it was, ma'am,' I rejoined.

"The old lady kissed her hand, gave another skip, smirked and sidled down the gallery in a most extraordinary manner, and ambled gracefully into her own bedchamber."

One of the first, if not actually the first, female centenarians in New England was Anne Pollard, who lived to be one hundred and five. She also had the distinction of being the first white woman to stand on the soil of Boston. As the boat neared the beach, she declared she would be the first one of her sex to land and leaped ashore from the bow of the boat before anyone else. She was a young girl at the time. The Massachusetts Historical Society has a portrait of her painted when she was one hundred and three, in which she looks like the traditional nursery-tale picture of Old Mother Hubbard.

it was thought proper to communicate them to the public."

At Bethel, Connecticut, not far from Stratford, is buried Joice Heth, the aged colored woman, whom Phineas T. Barnum exploited when a young man. The Yankee showman claimed that Joice had been a slave of Augustine Washington, the father of George Washington, and that she was one hundred and sixty-one years old. Not only was she present when the father of our country was born, but she had been the first to put clothes on him and had practically brought up "dear little George," as she always called him.

When Joice was exhibited at Niblo's Garden in New York, Barnum, in ballyhooing the ancient nurse, said, "She is cheerful and healthy, although she weights but forty-nine pounds. She relates many anecdotes of her young master; she also speaks of the red-coats during the Revolutionary War, but does not appear to hold them in high estimation. She has been visited by crowds of ladies and gentlemen, among whom were many clergymen and physicians, who have pronounced her the most ancient specimen of mortality the oldest of them has ever seen or heard of, and consider her a very great curiosity."

Joice sang hymns, smoked a corncob pipe, and

answered many questions about the Washingtons. People were apparently convinced that she was not a fake, and many more would have seen her but for the fact that not long after Barnum began exploiting her Joice was inconsiderate enough to die. This was in February, 1836, and Barnum had her buried in his native town of Bethel. In the opinion of the surgeons, who at Barnum's request performed an autopsy on her, the old Negress was not one hundred and sixty-one, but only about half that age. M. R. Werner, Barnum's biographer, says that as Barnum himself grew older he grew to be ashamed of the Joice Heth hoax.

In 1834 an aged colored prisoner died in the Connecticut State Prison at Wethersfield. He was Prince Mortimer, usually called Old Guinea, who served a life sentence for murder and was supposed to be one hundred and ten years old when he died. He served the first part of his sentence at Newgate Prison in East Granby, where at night he was confined below ground in the old copper mine. He was one of the sad procession of felons transferred to Wethersfield when the prison was completed in 1827.

The historian of Newgate says that Old Guinea when a boy was captured on the coast of Guinea by a slaver and was transported in a filthy slave ship to Connecticut, then a slave colony, where he was sold to one of the Mortimer family in Middletown. He was servant to different officers in the Revolutionary War. He claimed to have been sent on errands by General Washington and boasted that he had straddled many a cannon when fired by the Americans at British troops. For the alleged crime of poisoning his master he was doomed, in 1811, to Newgate Prison for life. He appeared a harmless, clever old man, and as his age and infirmities rendered him a burden to the keepers, they frequently tried to induce him to quit the prison. Once, he took his departure and, after rambling around in search of someone he formerly knew, like the aged prisoner released from the Bastille, he returned to the gates of the prison and begged to be readmitted to his dungeon home.

If Old Guinea was one hundred and ten when he died in 1834, he was eighty-seven when convicted of murder in 1811, which makes his case one of rather belated adventure in crime, but there was an advantage in this. The very old, like the very young, usually escape the gallows.

One occasionally reads of a modern centenarian spending his hundredth birthday at his office, but the experience of the elderly Connecticut gentleman who was sentenced to be hung the day he should be one hundred and who actually lived until the fatal day must surely be unique. Did he welcome the reprieve that was granted him on his birthday? With what spirit does a man at the age of one hundred face the prospect of life imprisonment? The centenarian in question was a man named Salisbury, from whom the town of Salisbury in the northwestern corner of Connecticut, near the New York border, is alleged to have derived its name, though it is also said that it was named after the English town of Salisbury in Wiltshire. In any case, the man Salisbury was one of the town of Salisbury's first settlers. The Rev. J. W. Crossman in his New Year's address delivered there in 1803 had this to say of the tough old man:

"It is currently reported, and by good authority, that this Mr. Salisbury, after moving from here, had an unruly servant girl who had run away from him; that he went after her, bound her with a rope, and tied her to his horse, then rode so as to pull her down, and drawed her in such a cruel manner that she died in consequence of the abuse. The matter was taken up in the state of New York, and he, then in old age, was sentenced by the court to be hung when he should be a hundred years old. About four years ago, he arrived to this age. A reprieve was granted him for a certain time; and if he has not died lately, he is living to this day."

Massachusetts also had a problem "centurion" in a Scotchman named Donald McDonald. Most centenarians like to attribute their longevity to a life of abstinence from intoxicants and from over indulgence of all kinds, but Donald McDonald was unblushingly fond of liquor, and because of his craving for alcohol had often to be assisted in the streets by kindhearted policemen, who sometimes had to take him to headquarters in a wheelbarrow. In September, 1825, the *Boston Courier* copied the following item from the *Salem Observer*:

"*Police Court.* Donald McDonald, a Scotchman reported to be 103 years of age, was brought before the court yesterday charged with being a common drunkard, of which he had been convicted once before. Donald stated that he had been in various battles of the Revolution, and had sailed with Paul Jones, and was at the taking of Quebec. He was found guilty and sentenced to the House of Correction for three months."

Four years later Donald was going stronger than ever in Boston, where he managed to get his name in the paper again and himself into jail. In 1829 the *Boston Patriot* reported as follows:

"Donald McDonald, the Scotchman, who has numbered upward of 107 years, was sent to the House of Industry on Saturday of last week, in a state of intoxication. He had been suffered to go at large but four days previous, and during two of them was seen about our streets a drunken brawler."

Death has for protracted periods of time overlooked many people in Maine. Chief Orono of the Penobscot Indians is an example. He was one hundred and thirteen when he died at Old Town in 1801. His quaint epitaph reads:

> Safe lodged within his blanket, here below,
> Lies the last relics of old Orono;
> Worn down with care, he in a trice
> Exchanged his wigwam for a paradise.

In the ancient German Protestant Cemetery at Waldoboro, Maine, is a public monument to Conrad Heyer, the grand old man of the town, who was born April 10, 1749, and died February 19, 1856, aged one hundred and six years, ten months, and nine days. "Conrad Heyer was the first child born of European parents in Waldoboro," reads the inscription on the monument. "He served three years in the Revolutionary War. This monument is erected by citizens of Waldoboro to perpetuate the memory of an honest and worthy man."

Conrad Heyer's father, Martin Heyer, died from hunger and exposure during the winter immediately preceding the birth of his son. He is the only one of the original settlers who came in 1748 whose name is now known. On another public monument in the same cemetery the interesting history of Waldoboro's establishment is summarized in these words:

"This town was settled in 1748 by Germans who emigrated to this place with the promise and expectation of finding a populous city, instead of which they found nothing but a wilderness; for the first few years they suffered to a great extent by Indian wars and starvation; by perseverance and self denial they succeeded in clearing lands and erecting mills. At the time a large proportion of the inhabitants are descendants of the first settlers. This monument was erected A.D. 1855 by the subscriptions of the citizens of the town."

A curious statement concerning a woman centenarian in the adjoining town of Bremen is made in Varney's *Gazetteer of the State of Maine* (1881). "Mrs. Mercy Studley, a resident of this town was, in 1880, one hundred and two years of age—one hundred and six, she herself says." So reads the statement, and one cannot help wondering why the the gazetteerist should give the old lady the lie direct. Is there a point at which women begin adding years to their age instead of subtracting them, and was the gazetteerist rebuking her for this? Living in the town next to Waldoboro, Mrs. Studley must have known of Conrad Heyer's record, and it may be that for the glory of her own town of Bremen she was determined at all costs to equal or better his score. Light might be shed on the matter by ascertaining the dates on her gravestone, although these are not always reliable, as we know from the case of Elizabeth Barrett Browning, who was so sensitive about being six years older than her husband that when she died the grief-stricken Robert deliberately falsified the date on her stone.

In 1860 the last survivor of the Battle of Bunker Hill was living in Acton, Maine. This was Ralph Farnham, who was then one hundred and four years old. The old gentleman was not a native of Maine, but of New Hampshire, and his birthday was celebrated by the people of Milton Mills, New Hampshire, with the firing of guns and other demonstrations. A person who visited him at Acton in September, 1860, said that as a result of the publicity given to the celebration at Milton Mills in July, Mr. Farnham had been deluged with requests for his autograph. Enlisting in the Revolutionary Army at the age of nineteen, Ralph Farnham had reached Cambridge just in time to take part in the Battle of Bunker Hill. He subsequently served with the army through three successive campaigns, from

1775 to 1777, and was on guard at the camp in Saratoga when Burgoyne surrendered to Gates.

John Gilley of West Augusta, Maine, who died in 1842 at the age of one hundred and twenty-four, was probably New England's oldest man. He did not marry until he was eighty, but he had ten children, the youngest of whom at his death was more than one hundred years younger than old John. He enjoyed sound and perfect teeth practically all his life. Shortly before he died, his hair, which had been a pure silvery white, turned black. Like other remarkably old men, he attracted many visitors.

The best portrait extant of a New England centenarian is the account by Timothy Dwight of his interview with Ephraim Pratt of Shutesbury, Massachusetts, who, though he did not live so long as John Gilley, was one of the oldest men New England has produced. Dwight, who rode ten miles out of his way to call on the old man, tells of the visit in his *Travels*.

"We arrived late in the afternoon," he says, "and found the object of our curiosity. He was born at Sudbury in 1687; and in one month from the date of our arrival would complete his one hundred and sixteenth year. He was of middle stature; firmly built; plump, but not encumbered with flesh; less withered than multitudes at seventy; possessed of considerable strength, as was evident from the grasp of his hand, and the sound of his voice; and without any marks of extreme age. About two months before, his sight became so impaired, that he was unable to distinguish persons. His hearing, also, for a short time had been so imperfect, that he could not distinctly hear common conversation. His memory was still vigorous; his understanding sound; and his mind sprightly in its conceptions.

"The principal part of the time, which I was in the house, he held me by the hand; cheerfully answered all my questions; readily gave me an account of himself in such particulars as I wished to know; observed to me that my voice indicated that I was not less than forty-five years of age; and that he must appear very old to me; adding, however, that some men, who had not passed their seventieth year, probably looked almost, or quite, as old as himself. The remark was certainly just, but it was the first time, that I had heard persons, who had reached the age of seventy, considered as being young. We were informed, partly by himself and partly by his host, that he had been a laborious man all his life; and particularly, that he had mown grass one hundred and one years successively. The preceding summer he had been unable to perform this labor. During this season his utmost effort was a walk of half a mile. In this walk he stumbled over a log, and fell. Immediately afterwards he began evidently to decline, and lost in a considerable degree both his sight and hearing. In the summer of 1802, he walked without inconvenience two miles, and mowed a small quantity of grass.

"Throughout his life he had been uniformly temperate. Ardent spirits he rarely tasted; cider he drank at times, but sparingly. In the vigorous periods of life he had accustomed himself to eat flesh, but much more abstemiously than most other persons in this country. Milk, which had always been a great part, was now the whole of his diet. He is naturally cheerful, and humorous, apparently unsusceptible of tender emotions, and not much inclined to serious thinking. According to an account, which he gave his host, he made a public profession of religion nearly seventy years before our visit to him; but was not supposed by him, nor by others acquainted with him, to be a religious man. He conversed easily, and was plainly gratified with the visits and conversation of strangers. When he was ninety-three years old he made a bargain with his host (who told us the story), that he should support him during the remainder of his life for £20.

"He was never sick but once, and then with the fever and ague. It is scarcely necessary to observe, that a man one hundred and sixteen years old, without religion, was a melancholy sight to me.

"Three or four months before this time I saw in a newspaper an advertisement, written by a person, who professed and appeared to be acquainted with him and his concerns, in which it was said, that his dependents, some of whom were of the fifth generation, amounted probably to more than fifteen hundred."

It is fortunate that Timothy Dwight went to see Ephraim Pratt that November afternoon, because shortly afterward the old fellow died. He was one hundred and sixteen when this occurred in 1804. He was a grandson of Joshua Pratt, one of the first planters at Plymouth.

Many other descendants of the Pilgrim Fathers lived to be immensely old. Elder John Faunce, of the first generation from the firstcomers, was all but a centenarian when he died at Plymouth in 1745, at the age of ninety-nine. His daughter, Patience Kempton, was one hundred and five and a half when she died at New Bedford in 1779. Ebenezer Cobb, of the third generation, was one hundred and seven years and eight months old when he passed away at Kingston in the year 1801. Peregrine White, the first English child born in New England, died at Marshfield in 1704, aged eighty-three. A grandson of Governor Carver lived in this town to the age of one hundred and two. In 1775 he was at work in the same field with his son, grandson, and great grandson, who had also an infant son in the house, making five generations.

Considering the hardships of the early days, many of the Pilgrim Fathers themselves did not do so badly, as is disclosed by the following table of the ages of some of those who arrived at Plymouth before 1631. Of those whose names appear in the list, Thomas Clark, the hardy mate of the "Mayflower," with a score of ninety-eight, comes closest to the century mark. Others whose records are not known may have lived as long or longer than those whose names are included.

Time of Decease		Age
1664	William Brewster	80
1664	Julia Kempton (*widow of Manasses*)	81
1667	Gabriel Hallowell	83
1668	John Downham (*Deacon*)	80
1670	Alice Bradford (*widow of the Governor*)	80
1672	John Howland	80
1673	Thomas Prince	73

Time of Decease		Age
1673	ELIZABETH WARREN (*widow of Richard*)	90
1675	ANN TUPPER (*Sandwich*)	97
1675	DOROTHY BROWN (*Swanzey*)	90
1676	THOMAS TUPPER (*Sandwich*)	97
1678	EDWARD BANGS (*Eastham*)	86
1685	NATHANIEL MORTON (*Secretary*)	73
1687	ROBERT FINNEY (*Deacon*)	80
1683	MARY CARPENTER	90
1689	GEORGE WATSON	86
1689	PRISCILLA COOPER	91
1691	THOMAS CUSHMAN (*Elder*)	84
1692	JOHN DOWNHAM (*son of the Deacon*)	79
1697	THOMAS CLARK (*mate of the "Mayflower"*)	98
1699	MARY CUSHMAN (*widow of the Elder*)	90
1704	GEORGE BONHAM	95
1705	SAMUEL KING	90
1710	PHEBE FINNEY (*widow of the Deacon*)	91
1688	SAMUEL EDDY	87
1682	ELIZABETH EDDY	81

Further instances of longevity among the first settlers in Massachusetts and other New England colonies are:

In Massachusetts

	Age
Richard Bellingham	82
Ezekiel Chever	94
Simon Bradstreet	94
Rev. John Higginson	93
Rev. John Elliot	86
Rev. Thomas Mayhew	93
Rev. Thomas Parker	82
President Chauncey	82
Rev. Nehemiah Walter	84
Rev. John Ward	88
Rev. Samuel Whiting	83
Rev. John Woodbridge	82

In Rhode Island

	Age
Roger Williams	84
Samuel Gorton	80
William Coddington	78

In Connecticut

	Age
Rev. James Fitch	80
Major John Mason	78

The Rev. Samuel Newman, founder of the town of Rehoboth, Massachusetts, had a premonition of his death, which occurred under dramatic circumstances in 1663, when he was a very old man. A person of great learning and piety, Mr. Newman was the author of a concordance of the Bible published in folio form in London in 1643, the year before his settlement at Rehoboth. Later he revised and enlarged the volume, working on it nights by the light of pine knots instead of candles, according to President Stiles of Yale College.

"The manner of his death," says Eliot, "was peculiar. He had a certain premonition of it, and seemed to triumph in the prospect of it being near. He was apparently in perfect health, and preached a sermon from these words, Job xiv: 14: '*All the days of my appointed time will I wait till my change come.*' In the afternoon of the following Lord's day he asked the deacon to pray with him, saying he had not long to live. As soon as he had finished his prayer, he said the time was come when he must leave the world; but his friends, seeing no immediate signs of dissolution, thought it was the influence of imagination. But he turned round, saying, 'Angels, do your office!' and immediately expired."

TO EXCEL IN EPITAPHS

THE custom of writing verses in memory of the dead in the form of elegies and epitaphs did not originate in New England, but it flourished there from the seventeenth century until the last quarter of the last century. It constituted an important outlet for the widespread passion which people have for writing poetry. The fashion for these verses seems to have reached its height before the Civil War, in what may be called the weeping-willow period of American literature and art.

During that period so many poetical obituaries dripped from the pen of Lydia Huntley Sigourney, the Hartford poetess, that she was said to have added a new terror to death. No prominent mediocrity could die without Mrs. Sigourney tossing off some fulsomely eulogistic lines about the helpless dead one. She was especially fond of writing verses about children nipped in the bud and, as the rate of infant mortality was then very high, she had plenty of opportunities to indulge this bent. While many a poet found that the only way he could get his verse before the public was to have it carved on stone in the local churchyard, Mrs. Sigourney had no difficulty in getting her poetry published. Her work was enormously popular. No keepsake or annual of the time was highly esteemed unless it contained a bit of pensive sentiment from her pen. In much of this verse she very sweetly directed the thoughts of her readers to the grave.

Our concern here, however, is not with the printed elegies, but rather with the epitaphs and other inscriptions which were brief enough to be cut in stone with maul and chisel. Even the most neglected New England burial places yield quaint epitaphs, apt quotations, and striking scriptural allusions, to say nothing of the grinning death's-heads, urns, weeping willows, and other examples of old-fashioned mortuary sculpture. Oddly shaped monuments are also to be found occasionally. Inquiry concerning an antique knocker on the door of a curious old tomb revealed a tradition that it had been placed there so that the family inside would know when the Old Nick called and could say they were not at home and escape by the back door.

Many epitaphs in the coastal and river burial grounds are above the graves of seafaring men and are appropriately of a nautical nature. One of these which occurs in widely separated places, in slightly different readings, is the following from the monument of Captain E. Griffen at Madison, Connecticut:

> Though Boreas' blasts and Neptune's waves
>   Have toss'd me to and fro,
> In spite of both by God's decree
>   I harbor here below,
> Where I do at anchor ride
>   With many of our fleet;
> Yet once again I must set sail
>   Our Admiral, Christ, to meet.

At East Hampton, Connecticut, is another nautical inscription on the tombstone of a seaman who died in 1883 at the age of eighty-seven.

Landsmen or sailors
For a moment avast,
Poor Jack's main topsail
Is laid to the mast,
The worms gnaw his timbers,
His vessel a wreck,
When the last whistle sounds
He'll be up on deck.

Over the grave of a fisherman on Cape Cod is this appropriate inscription:

Capt. Thomas Coffin
Born Jan. 7, 1792. Died Jan. 10, 1842
He has finished catching cod,
And gone to meet his God.

An interesting piece of marine history is preserved on the stone of another old salt, Freeman Hatch, at Eastham on Cape Cod. "In 1852 he became famous making the astonishing passage in the clipper ship Northern Light from Frisco to Boston in 76 days, 6 hours, an achievement won by no other mortal before or since."

A tragedy of the sea is recalled by an inscription on a monument at Attleboro, Massachusetts, which reads: "In memory of Dr. Herbert Mann, who with 119 sailors, with Capt. James Magee, master, went on board the Brig General Arnold in Boston Harbor 25th Dec. 1778, hoisted sail, made for sea, and were immediately overtaken by the most tremendous snow storm with cold, that was ever known in the memory of man, and unhappily parted their cable in Plymouth Harbor, in a place called the Cow-yards, and he with about 100 others was frozen to death; sixty-six of whom were buried in one grave. He was in the 21st year of his age. And now Lord God Almighty, just and true are all thy ways, but who can stand before thy cold?"

But the prize epitaph on death in the deep is one at Kittery, Maine, which states the facts in four lines.

I was drowned, alas! in the deep, deep seases.
The blessed Lord does as he pleases.
But my Kittery friends did soon appear,
And laid my body right down here.

Many accidental deaths on land, some of them caused by horses, are also recorded on old New England tombstones. One of the choicest of equine epitaphs is a quatrain on a stone at Oxford, New Hampshire, which reads:

To all my friends I bid adieu,
  A more sudden death you never knew.
As I was leading the old mare to drink.
  She kicked and killed me quicker'n a wink.

The full story of the tragic death of a horseman is told on a tombstone at Montague, Massachusetts, in these words: "Elijah Bardwell, died Jan 26, 1786, aged 27 years, having but a few days survived ye fatal night when he was flung from his horse, and drawn by ye stirrups 26 rods along ye path, as appeared by the place where his hat was found, and here he spent the whole of ye following severe cold night, treading down the snow in a small circle. The family he left was an aged father, a wife and three small children."

The Rev. Bunker Gay of Hinsdale, New Hampshire, wrote an epitaph for Jonathan Tute, who died from the effects of inoculation and was buried in Vernon, Vermont. Some of the lines which have made persons pause beside the unfortunate Jonathan's grave and ponder his sad fate read as follows:

Here lies cut down, like unripe fruit,
A son of Mr. Amos Tute.

* * * *

To death he fell a helpless prey,
On April V and Twentieth Day,
In Seventeen Hundred Seventy-Seven
Quitting this world, we hope, for heaven.

Behold the amazing alteration,
Effected by inoculation;
The means empowered his life to save,
Hurried him headlong to the grave.

The fear inspired by smallpox was such that when a young hatter named Fisher Hartshorn was stricken with the disease and died a few days after his arrival in the town of Woodbury, Connecticut, near Danbury, the local authorities, fearing the spread of the contagion, refused to permit the youthful stranger to be buried in the town cemetery, even though his brethren of the Society of Hatters offered to do it at midnight. The members of the society buried Hartshorn in a lonely grave near the old house in which he was isolated when he broke out with the disease. With a spirit honorable to themselves and the society to which they belonged, the hatters not only buried their colleague but raised a monument to his memory. The inscription reads:

"This monument erected by the Society of Hatters, to the memory of their brother, *Fisher Hartshorn*, a native of Charlestown, Mass., who fell a victim to the small pox, and was buried in this place, Feb. 1825, aged 21 years.

In this retired and lonely grave,
The stranger is at rest;
His spirit gone to him who gave,
To dwell among the blest."

Records of crime are carved on stone in many old skull orchards. Some of these inscriptions, like the headlines of newspapers, tell a fairly full story in remarkably few words. An inscription like the following from a tombstone at Brookfield, Massachusetts, is enough to arouse any reader's curiosity.

Joshua Spooner
Murdered Mar. 1, 1778,
by three soldiers of the
Revolution,
Ross, Brooks and Buchanan,
at the instigation of
his wife Bathsheba.
They were all executed
at Worcester,
July 2, 1778.

According to a memorial at Wethersfield, Connecticut, one of the guards at the state prison was murdered by convicts in 1833. "This stone, erected by the State," says the inscription, "is in memory of Ezra Hoskins, aged 66, whose remains lie beneath it. In an insurrection of convicts, he was inhumanly killed on the night following the 30th of April, 1833, at midnight on duty as a patrole, in the State Prison. He ended an useful and inoffensive life, by a most tragical death."

Also at Wethersfield is the record of the destruction of a whole family in a shocking series of ax murders committed by an insane man who then killed himself. It reads: "Here lies interred Mrs. Lydia Beadle, aged 32 years. Ansell, Lothrop, Elizabeth, Lydia and Mary Beadle, her children. The oldest aged 11 years, the youngest 6 years. Who on the morning of the 11th of Dec. A. D. 1782, fell by the hands of William Beadle, an infuriated man, who closed the horrid sacrifice of his wife and children with his own destruction.

Pale round their grassy tombs bedew'd with tears,
Flit the thin forms of sorrows and of fears;
Soft sighs responsive swell to plaintive chords,
And Indignations half unsheath their swords."

A serious charge was brought against the widow of a man in Pelham, Massachusetts, when the dead man's brother caused the following inscriptions to be cut on his gravestone:

Warren Gibbs,
Died by arsenic poison
March 23, 1860 Aged 36 years
5 months and 23 days
Think my friends when this you see
How my wife has dealt by me
She in some oysters did prepare
Some poison for my lot and share
Then of the same I did partake
And nature yielded to its fate
Before she my wife became
Mary Felton was her name.
Erected by his brother
Wm Gibbs

The widow apparently was neither tried for murder, nor did she sue the author of the epitaph for libel. The present stone is said to be a duplicate of one which the widow's relatives demolished.

The following curious epitaph on a young woman is from East Hartford, Connecticut:

Now she is dead and cannot stir;
  Her cheeks are like the faded rose;
Which of us next shall follow her,
  The Lord Almighty only knows.

Hark, she bids all her friends adieu;
  An angel calls her to the spheres;
Our eyes the radiant saint pursue
  Through liquid telescopes of tears.

Another queer epitaph on a young woman is at Dorchester, Massachusetts.

On the 21st of March
God's angels made a sarche.
Around the door they stood;
They took a maid,
It is said,
And cut her down like wood.

A child named Emily has the following epitaph in Mount Auburn Cemetery:

Shed not for her the bitter tear,
  Nor give the heart to vain regret;
Tis but the casket that lies here:
  The gem that filled it sparkles yet.

Two children at Waterbury, Connecticut, who were burned to death February 25, 1833, are memorialized in this epitaph:

The midnight fire was fierce and red,
Sweet babes that wrapt your sleeping bed—
But He who oft with favoring ear
Hath bow'd, your early prayers to hear,
Received beyond this mortal shore,
The sister souls to part no more.

Above the grave of a young woman who died at Milford, Connecticut, in 1792, at the age of twenty-four, are these grim lines:

Molly, tho' pleasant in her day,
Was sudd'nly seized and sent away.
How soon she's ripe, how soon she's rotten,
Laid in the grave and soon forgott'n.

Unique and ludicrous is the verse on a Connecticut man with a remarkable tumor.

Our father lies beneath the sod,
His spirit's gone unto his God;
We never more shall hear his tread,
Nor see the wen upon his head.

Another New England graveyard inscription which is often quoted reads:

Here lies John Auricular,
Who in the ways of the Lord walked perpendicular.

One class of epitaphs often found in New England comprises those of a financial or business character. Near the eastern boundary of Connecticut is the grave of a Rhode Island man, who, according to the statement on his tombstone, refused to be buried in his native state because it had repudiated a debt. It is not unusual to find on gravestones the amount of money left by the deceased to charity. These financial statements were generally the work of the executors, but their aim was undoubtedly to say something which would have been pleasing to the deceased.

Captain Thomas Prentice, the partisan commander of horse, so distinguished in King Phillip's War, died in 1709 at the age of eighty-nine in consequence of a fall from his horse. The following lines were deciphered from the footstone of his grave at Newton, Massachusetts:

He that's here interred needs no versifying,
A virtuous life will keep the name from dying;
He'll live, though poets cease their scribbling
rhyme,
When that this stone shall moulder'd be by time.

From Tewksbury, Massachusetts, comes this saintly one:

> Here lies Mr. William Wood,
> Who while he lived was very good,
> But now he is dead and gone above,
> To see the Lord he dearly loved.

The descendants of a man at Searsport, Maine, are said to have had so much fun poked at them on account of the following epitaph that they had it effaced:

> Under the sod and under the trees
> Here lies the body of Solomon Pease
> The Pease are not here there's only the pod
> The Pease shelled out and went to God.

John Abbot of Andover, Massachusetts, who died in 1793 at the age of ninety, has this moralizing epitaph:

> Grass, smoke, a flower, a vapor, a shade, a span,
> Serve to illustrate the frail life of man;
> And they, who longest live, survive to see
> The certainty of death, of life the vanity.

At Attleboro, Massachusetts, an aged Negro is commemorated in these lines:

Here lies the best of slaves,
  Now turning into dust.
Caesar, the Ethiopian, craves
  A place among the just.
His faithful soul is fled
  To realms of heavenly light;
And by the blood that Jesus shed,
  Is changed from black to white.

Major General Humphry Atherton had a fine funeral when he was buried at Dorchester, Massachusetts, in 1661. He was killed after a military review, when his horse collided with a cow on Boston Common and threw him.

Here lyes our captaine, and major of Suffolk was withall,
A goodly magistrate was he, and major generall.
Two troops of hors with him here came, such worth his love did crave,
Ten companyes of foot also mourning marcht to his grave.
Let all that read be sure to keep the faith as he has don;
With Christ he lives now crowned. His name was Humphry Atherton.

Also at Dorchester is an acrostical epitaph to the memory of Elder James Humphrey, whose death occurred in 1686.

I nclosed within this shrine is precious dust,
A nd only waits the rising of the just;
M ost useful while he lived, adorned his station,
E ven to old age served his generation,
S ince his decease thought of with veneration.

H ow great a blessing this ruling elder he
U nto this church and town and pastors three!
M ather, the first, did by him help receive;
F lint he did next his burden much relieve;
R enowned Danforth did he assist with skill,
E steemed high above all, bear fruit until,
Y ielding to death, his glorious seat did fill.

Many of the eulogies engraved on marble in honor of the dead are probably more the description of what would have been desirable in their characters than a faithful record of what they actually were in life. Some of the most highly eulogistic epitaphs are those of the ministers of the New England churches, but one feels that these men merited the good that was said of them. Here is one from Quincy, Massachusetts, dated 1708:

Braintree, thy prophet's gone; this tomb inters
The Rev. Moses Fiske his sacred herse.
Adore heaven's praiseful art, that formed the man,
Who souls, not to himself, but Christ oft won;
Sailed through the straits with Peter's family
Renowned, and Gaius' hospitality,
Paul's patience, James's prudence, John's sweet love,
Is landed, entered, cleared, and crowned above.

At Watertown, Massachusetts, is the following epitaph which reads like a catalogue:

Here lyes the precious dust of Thomas Bailey

A painful preacher, A most desirable neighbor,
An eminent liver, A pleasant companion,
A tender husband, A common good,
A careful father, A cheerful doer,
A brother of adversity, A patient sufferer,
A faithful friend, Lived much in little time.
A good copy for all survivors.

Quite as effective is this short one from Barnstable, Massachusetts, from the tombstone of the Rev. Joseph Green, who died in 1770 at the age of three score years and ten.

Think what the Christian minister should be,
You've seen his character, for such was he.

Of later vintage are the two following epitaphs which I have been unable to trace. They may not be genuine, but I have heard them all my life, and they have the true New England flavor. The first one reads as follows:

> Here lies the body of Saphronia Proctor,
> Who had a cold, but wouldn't doctor.
> She couldn't stay, she had to go,
> Praise God from whom all blessings flow.

The second epitaph also tells a tale of negligence that proved fatal.

> Beneath this little mound of clay
> Lies Captain Ephraim Daniels,
> Who chose the dangerous month of May
> To change his winter flannels.

In New London County, Connecticut, is the burial lot of a man who had four wives. At each corner of the lot is a stone, the first marked "Wife I," the next "Wife II," the third "Wife III," and the last "Wife IV." In the center is a large monument bearing the words, "Our Husband."

Another Connecticut patriarch who was blessed with a quartet of wives had inscribed over the grave of the last one, "She was the best of all."

Curious things have appeared on gravestones besides epitaphs. On the tombstone of Colonel Jonathan Buck of Bucksport, Maine, is the likeness of a woman's leg, which has defied all attempts to obliterate it. It is known locally as the Witch's Curse. Legend says that before moving from Massachusetts to Maine, Colonel Buck officiated at the execution of a witch who put a curse on him.

Several years ago a New Hampshire woman, who buried her husband and settled down to a quiet widowhood, was startled by the appearance on her husband's tombstone of a likeness of his first wife. It made her wonder what was going on in the spirit world.

TO THIRST AFTER STRANGE GODS

ORIGINATING and organizing new religious sects has always been a favorite New Eng-
and pastime. Strange creeds, some of them brand
iew, others very old and revived, have cropped up
ike weeds, and no matter how noxious or far-
etched they were, all seem to have succeeded in
ittracting at least a few adherents. Most of them,
of course, proved short-lived. They had their little
lay and ceased to be. Their brief chronicles are

scattered through the town histories of the region.

From the history of Sutton, Massachusetts, for example, one learns that there once existed in that town a sect known as the Live for Evers. They thought that if you seemed to be dead, faith accompanied by certain manipulations by the faithful would restore you to life, and this part of their faith is what gave them their name. But they had other views of a more original and peculiar kind. They believed that, like Adam, every man had a wife made from one of his own ribs, and there was great danger of trouble if he got the wrong one for his spouse, though it is not clear how he was expected to know the right one when he met her. Evidently it was purely a matter of trial and error.

At any rate, the female Live for Evers had definite ideas on this point, for some of them got the notion that they were misplaced and carried the idea to the extent of misplacing themselves in their own beds by putting the pillow for the man at one end and that for the woman at the other. Some even went beyond this and, becoming dissatisfied with their mates, sought their affinities. To discuss and adjust their difficulties they held evening meetings at each other's homes.

Among the restless ladies of the group were Mrs. Lucy Fletcher and her sister, Mrs. Miner. The latter ran away, but whether she went to her mother's or took to the road with some itinerant bellows mender, the record is silent. In any case, her husband pursued her, and it is said that it was only with the greatest difficulty that he persuaded her to return. As for her sister, Lucy Fletcher, her husband, Ebenezer, came home one rainy night to find the Live for Evers holding a meeting in his house. He had no sympathy with their views and ordered them to leave, but, pleading that it was raining, they refused to go, which made Mr. Fletcher very, very angry.

"If you fear rain more than fire," he cried, "you can stay." And, seizing the fire shovel, he began to throw hot embers and live coals from the fireplace around the room among the crowd. This rain of fire drove them from the house, and Ebenezer, having extinguished the brands, went to bed.

The sequel came a few days later when he went to the neighboring town of Grafton with his oxen and tipcart. From this journey Mr. Fletcher never returned alive, as he was found lying dead in the road, and it is supposed that he was murdered by the Live for Evers. No record of his death, however, could be found by the historians of Sutton, but the date of the marriage of his widow to John Goodale was discovered to have taken place on December 12, 1781, and this, perhaps, is as near as it is possible to place the unfortunate Ebenezer in historic time.

In the tenets of many sects that have attracted attention and adherents there has been a tincture of free love. This was the case with a sect called the Dorrellites, which once existed in the town of Leyden, near Greenfield, Massachusetts. The name of the order came from its founder, William Dorrell, a native of England, who was born on a farm in Yorkshire, March 15, 1752. When a young man, Dorrell became a soldier, serving in several campaigns in Ireland, after which he came to America, where his military career was terminated when he was captured with Gentleman Johnny Burgoyne at Saratoga in 1777. For a time he lived in Petersham, Massachusetts, where he fell in love with and married a girl ten years younger than himself named Polly Chase. He then moved to Warwick, and finally, in 1784, to Leyden, which was the scene of his rise and fall.

Dorrell was illiterate and intemperate, but he was a remarkable person. He was a handsome man six feet or more in height, with a very pleasing manner. He had fine native ability, great firmness of mind, and an exceptionally retentive memory. He could neither read nor write, but he knew large portions of the Bible by heart from hearing his wife read it. His power of attraction is shown by the fact that his followers were not just ignorant country folk but included some of the most intelligent and respectable churchgoing people of Leyden and Bernardston, among them several town officials. Despite Dorrell's liking for strong drink, he had the reputation in his own community of being punctual in the fulfillment of his engagements, whether drunk or sober. He does not seem to have been personally interested in money, which apparently flowed freely into the Dorrellite treasury, for the historian of Bernardston, writing in 1902, says an astute businessman handled the finances, and it was common gossip that the money belonging to the sect was the foundation of the fortune of one of the wealthiest families in that part of Massachusetts.

Dorrell, who began to have followers in the spring of 1794, had little use for the Bible. His first revelation came to him, he said, while he was chopping wood. He could not remember it exactly, but it was something like, "Render yourself an acceptable sacrifice." One of his principal doctrines was that no one should cause the death of any living thing. Eating flesh or using the skins of animals for any domestic purposes was forbidden to his followers. Consequently, the Dorrellites did not wear leather shoes, nor did they use harness made of leather for their horses. Most of them wore wooden shoes made locally by Ezra Shattuck, one of their number, and substituted rope harness for leather harness for their animals. The leather bellows of Amos Burroughs, the village blacksmith, presented a problem, but Mr. Burroughs solved it satisfactorily by camouflaging the leather with painted cloth. The bulk of the membership wore clothing made of a coarse tow cloth.

Dorrell believed in nonresistance and personal immunity for the faithful from bodily harm. He would say, "No arm of flesh can hurt me." He was no Sabbatarian, holding that all days were alike, one as sacred as another, and the Dorrellites met on any day that happened to suit them. Seven of them were prosecuted for raising a house on the Sabbath, but a lawyer from Greenfield got all but one cleared of the charge. As Dorrell's curious doctrines spread through Leyden and the neighboring towns and people were attracted by them and joined him, he added new features to his religion, including freedom of love, and the later meetings of the cult are said to have become "scenes of the most outrageous and beastly conduct, interspersed with the singing of Bacchanalian songs and lascivious addresses."

The order reached its peak about 1798, by which time a score or more of families, some from

Bernardston, had cast in their lot with Dorrell. Families were large in those days and his followers were probably quite numerous.

That same year the Rev. John Taylor of Deerfield interviewed Dorrell for the purpose of obtaining directly from him a statement of his beliefs, and the following is the substance of what Dorrell told him.

"Every generation of men has its Messiah; that he (Dorrell) was the Messiah of his generation; that no arm of flesh could hurt him; that there was no resurrection from the dead; that when 'resurrection' was spoken of in the Bible its meaning was resurrection from a state of sin to spiritual life; that Jesus Christ was a spirit; that he took a body; that he died; but that he was never raised from the dead; that all who are raised from a state of sin to this spiritual life become perfect; that they can then do no sin, and are no more responsible to the civil law, and are beyond all principalities and powers. There was no future judgment, no knowledge after death of what passed in the world; that God had no power over man to control his actions, therefore there was no need for prayer. He had no hope for the future, but he had abundance of assurance that all was well. He was perfect, his body being in perfect obedience to the spirit, and his followers were comparatively perfect, as the members of the body are perfect when compared to the head; that all covenants made by God with man were ended, and he was the head of a new covenant; that neither Moses nor Christ wrought miracles, and that he stood precisely the same as Jesus Christ, and that while no person might worship his human body yet he might be worshipped as Christ was worshipped, God united to human flesh."

Concerning the scandalous conduct of the members resulting from the teaching that spiritual perfection made one sinless, Dorrell, according to Mr. Taylor, was extremely cautious and reticent. But on the subject of marriage, Dorrell said that when a husband or wife achieved perfection and one was raised to the spiritual life, the other party was released from the civil bonds of matrimony, and if both were raised, neither was beholden to the other, but both had a perfect right to promiscuous intercourse.

Dorrell's career as a religious leader was brought to an abrupt close and the sect liquidated in 1800. The last meeting was well attended, and, after opening it with music, Dorrell began to address the gathering, which was composed mostly of the faithful, though at least one of his listeners was not a Dorrellite. This was Captain Ezekial Foster, a giant of a man, who thought Dorrell a charlatan and his teachings bosh. When Dorrell in the course of his blasphemous and boasting address declared, "No arm of flesh can hurt me," the captain promptly refuted the statement by rising and knocking the seer down with his fist. Stunned and frightened, Dorrell struggled to his feet, only to receive a second blow, which made him cry for mercy. But the captain continued to beat him, declaring that he would not spare him until Dorrell renounced his infamous doctrines. None of the Dorrellites came to the aid of their leader, perhaps because they knew the captain could lick the whole crowd, and at length to save himself from further punishment, Dorrell agreed to recant. This he did to the amazement of his followers, saying he guessed he had led them a wild goose chase long enough. His followers, thoroughly disgusted, dispersed. And thus were the Dorrellites quenched.

Dorrell did not leave Leyden, as might have been expected, but lived out the long balance of his life there. In 1834 he was visited by Governor Cushing, who found him living in the northwest corner of the town in a poor, smoky, old house in a bleak place remote from any other habitation or traveled road. The furniture consisted of a table, a bed, a loom, crockery shelves, and two or three chairs. Although he was then in his eighties, the old impostor was in excellent health and boasted that he still got drunk occasionally. He had no followers, but clung to his religion, declaring that the Bible was all wrong. Nor did he think that Dorrellism was extinct. Some, he thought, still secretly cherished the religion, and it is true that none of his followers ever joined any other sects.

For several years before his death Dorrell was a town pauper. He died August 28, 1846, aged ninety-four years, five months, and thirteen days, having committed suicide by deliberately starving himself to death. He said he had lived long enough and that if he continued to eat he was afraid he would never die. His last act was a negation of his own pet doctrine of the absolute sanctity of life.

Force was also used to suppress another New England sect. Early in the nineteenth century the Rev. George Higgins, a Methodist minister of Carmel, Maine, started a cult which ended in his banishment from the town. His followers, who were known as Higginsites, did not eat pork and believed in healing by faith. There was nothing objectionable in this, but among the stories that were told of the Higginsites there was one that stirred the community to action. It was that Mr. Higgins used whips to drive the devil out of the children of his followers. This was more than the orthodox folk of the town could tolerate, and one night Mr. Higgins was summoned from his bed to receive a veneering of tar and feathers at the hands of the outraged Carmelites, who then ran him out of town.

Few things show the power of the old-time fanatical religious leaders better than their success in inducing whole sections of communities to sever all ties and follow them to fresh woods and pastures new. Schisms in the early churches were responsible for the establishment of many new settlements. A society would be torn by dissensions, perhaps over some minor point or points of doctrine, and the disaffected members would go off in a huff to found a new society and a new town of their own. But that was different from the case of the zealots who were personally ambitious and burned with the desire to establish little kingdoms of their own. To some of these adventurers religion was but a handmaiden serving to appease their vanity and lust for power. Others, of course, were honest, crusading souls with a mission. Of some it is difficult to say whether they were charlatans or not. In varying degrees all possessed qualities of leadership.

One of the most remarkable migrations from New England undertaken at the prompting of a religious adventurer occurred when the barkentine "Nellie Chapin" sailed from Jonesport, Maine, shortly after the Civil War, with a load of colonists bound for the Holy Land. The promoter of the expedition was an itinerant preacher, a dissatisfied Latter-day Saint from Philadelphia named G. J. Adams, who formed an organization called the Palestine Emigration Association. Mr. Adams must have been gifted beyond most preachers to persuade the hardheaded people of the Maine coast to sell everything they owned and join him in his crackpot scheme to redeem the Holy Land. For the idea underlying the venture was that of a peaceful crusade to build a new Palestine on the shabby and crumbling foundations of Moslem civilization. The Down-Easters were to form the spearhead of the new movement. Mr. Adams in his eloquent way practically promised them the gorgeous East in fee. When embarrassing questions were put to him as to how various practical problems were to be met, he gave such answers as, "The Lord will provide. Throw yourselves upon the Lord." And these answers apparently satisfied the people, because one day upward of one hundred and fifty men, women, and children from Jonesport and vicinity, including many from Beal's Island, put to sea with the visionary Mr. Adams in the "Nellie Chapin" and fifty-two days later reached Jaffa.

Near Jaffa, the seaport of Jerusalem, they actually established a colony. All was new and strange to them and, it must be owned, terribly disappointing. The place was not like the picture Mr. Adams had painted. Here was no earthly paradise flowing with milk and honey. The site of the colony was unhealthful. The flea-bitten natives pestered them. Hardships and harassments they had never dreamed of were experienced, and it did not help them in their misery to realize how badly they had been misled by Mr. Adams who, when he saw how things were going, took to drink. Under the circumstances it is not surprising that quarrels and dissensions should break out among the colonists. The situation, which had been hopeless from the first, went rapidly from bad to worse, and within a twelvemonth the colony disintegrated. The surviving exiles, after many difficulties and delays, were repatriated. The only bright spot in the whole haggard affair was that one of the colonists, with traditional Yankee enterprise, succeeded in starting a stage line between Jaffa and Jerusalem.

A sect of reformers calling themselves Christians created a good deal of excitement in Hampton, Connecticut, and adjoining towns early in the last century. They made so much noise at their meetings that they could be heard two miles away. To humble themselves and to become literally like little children, they used to creep or crawl about on the floor. In a spirit of detachment from worldly affairs they neglected to milk their cows or to perform other essential everyday tasks. Of the two men who were their leaders, one named Varnum seems to have exerted a strong influence over many of the members of the sect, a number of whom he persuaded to migrate with him to Ohio, where he proposed to establish an earthly paradise. Those who went were soon disillusioned, and Varnum himself turned Shaker, advising his companions to do likewise, which some of them did.

The Rogerenes were another wild and boisterous sect, who took their name from John Rogers of New London, the founder and leader of the movement. Rogers, an inordinately ambitious man, borrowed his aggressive tactics from two Quaker men —lewd fellows, according to Trumbull—who came singing and dancing through the colony. These men were accompanied by several women who assisted them in their exercises and from whose lips, it was claimed, dripped myrrh and honey. John Rogers, imbibing a generous measure of their spirit, became a convert to their religion. It is true that not long after he turned Seventh-Day Baptist, but a short time later he returned to Quakerism, or rather to his own personal version of it.

"To gratify his pride," says Dr. Trumbull in his

History of Connecticut, "and that he might appear as the head of a peculiar sect, he differed in several points from the Quakers. . . . To make himself more eminent, as the head of a new sect, he commenced preaching of his peculiar scheme, and, without any kind of ordination, administered baptism to his followers. The madness, immodesty and tumultuous conduct of Rogers and those who followed him, at this day, is hardly conceivable. It seemed to be their study and delight to violate the Sabbath. They would come, on the Lord's day, into the most public assemblies nearly or quite naked, and in the time of public worship, behave in a wild and tumultuous manner, crying out, and charging the most venerable ministers with lies and false doctrine. They would labor upon the Lord's day, drive carts by places of public worship, and from town to town, apparently on purpose to disturb Christians and Christian assemblies."

When hailed into court, Rogers would shout, scream, roar, stamp, and behave like a maniac, and then laugh at the sport he made for himself until his sides shook. He was divorced from his wife for fornication and supposed bestiality, to which, it is said, he confessed out of court. He purchased a girl whom he used to take to bed whenever it suited him and, after she had borne him two children, he put her out. He once sat upon the gallows on a conviction for blasphemy and underwent imprisonment for some time for having been an accomplice in the burning of the meetinghouse at New London.

The Rogerenes were like juvenile braggarts who take particular delight in flouting authority. They seemed to be at special pains to violate the law in the presence of officials, so they would be sure to be complained of and have the opportunity to show their contempt for the courts and claim they were being persecuted. One of their favorite violations was to take wives to themselves in defiance of all laws, but in this they were not always so smart as they thought they were.

One day when Governor Saltonstall was sitting in his room smoking his pipe, a Rogerene named Gurdon came in with a woman clinging to his arm and boldly addressed the governor.

"Sir," he said, "I have married this woman and that, too, without the authority of your magistrates and ministers."

The governor turned round and, taking his pipe from his mouth, said sternly, "Gurdon, have you taken this woman for your wife?"

"Yes, I have," Gurdon replied.

Then, turning to the woman, Governor Saltonstall asked, "Madam, have you taken this man for your husband?"

"Indeed, sir, I have," said the Rogerene woman.

"Well, then," said the governor, "by authority of and according to the laws of Connecticut I pronounce you man and wife."

Gurdon was speechless with astonishment, and then, "Thou art a cunning creature," he cried, as he left hurriedly with his bride.

Employment of physicians or the use of medicine in case of illness was against the tenets of the Rogerenes. During the terrible smallpox epidemic in Boston in 1721, John Rogers was confident that he could go there with perfect safety and to show his faith journeyed to Boston, where he exposed himself to the disease. It was a fatal mistake, for he caught smallpox, and, after returning home and giving it to his family, he died.

Unlike most sects, the Rogerenes carried on for years after the loss of their leader. As late as 1763 some of them clapped shingles and boards outside the meetinghouse in Norwich Town, and fully a century after John Rogers's death descendants of his followers still held other faiths in such low esteem that they would not work as carpenters or otherwise on the new church which was built at New London.

Cults like that of the Rogerenes and others mentioned here, which in earlier days sprang up like weeds all over New England, were largely attributable to the bleakness and austerity of New England life and the atmosphere of religious revivalism that frequently prevailed for long periods over the region. Something, too, in the Yankee character made New Englanders willing listeners to the bland and loquacious personalities from among their own numbers who exploited the situation by promising a new heaven and a new earth to all who would follow them. The fact that most of these cults collapsed after a short time did not discourage others from coming forward with plans for newer and better ones. Starting these movements became quite a custom, which it is not yet safe to pronounce dead, for New England gives up its old ways slowly and reluctantly.

TO HAVE HAUNTED HOUSES

ANOTHER old New England custom was that of the haunted house. There was a time when every town, village, and hamlet had its haunted residence, but most of them have vanished, perhaps because Yankees dislike having tenants who do not pay rent. One still hears occasionally of such places, but most of them prove as elusive and difficult to track down as the ghosts which are supposed to haunt them. Clues as to their whereabouts are too indefinite and shadowy to permit of location and identification. They are generally referred to vaguely as being "somewhere in Maine," or "high up on the watershed of the Connecticut," or "in a sequestered valley of the Berkshires." There are many deserted and derelict houses which imaginative children living in the neighborhood like to invest with the glamour of a ghost, but this is only make-believe, and these places are not genuine haunted houses, save in the sense alluded to by Longfellow when he said, "All houses wherein man has lived or died are haunted houses."

Although in the early days, particularly during the time of the witchcraft excitement, ghosts were personal rather than residential, haunted houses were not altogether unknown then. Increase Mather gives several instances in his *Remarkable Providences* (1684). One of the earliest cases was a house in Newbury belonging to one William Morse, which in 1679 was strangely disquieted by a demon. George Walton of Portsmouth and Nicholas Desborough of Hartford were also troubled by devils—non-human ones—in their homes. These cases had certain features in common, which set the basic pattern for many later hauntings. Stones, brickbats, and even chamber pots were hurled about recklessly, while the occupants of the houses were banged and shoved around in a very cruel and alarming way. Black cats sometimes figured in the early cases, and horseshoes nailed above doors were found to be antidotes against the molestations. Belief in witchcraft was widespread at the time, but Increase Mather admits that in one case there were some people who ascribed the strange incidents, not to supernatural powers but to a seaman who was suspected of being a conjurer. Yet, he hastens to add, it may have been "some other thing hid in the secrets of Providence that was the true original of the trouble."

Cotton Mather, the son of Increase, was as interested as his father in the wonders of the invisible world and rewrote one of the older man's reports of some strange doings at a house in New Hampshire, which he included in his *Magnalia Christi Americana.* Cotton, it will perhaps be recalled, was the Mather who described the Devil as a tawny fellow and said the streets of Boston reeked of brimstone. The report, which is typical of the Pilgrim period hauntings, reads as follows:

"In June, 1682, Mary the wife of Antonio Hortado, dwelling near the Salmon-Falls, heard a voice at the door of her house, calling, 'What do you here?' and about an hour after had a blow on her eye, that almost spoiled her. Two or three days after, a great stone was thrown along the house; which the people going to take up, was unaccountably gone. A frying pan then in the chimney rang so loud, that the people at an hundred rods distance heard it; and the said Mary with her husband, going over the river in a canoe, they saw the head of a man, and, about three feet off, the tail of a cat, swimming before the canoe, but no body to join them; and the same apparition again followed the canoe when they returned; but at their landing it first disappeared. A stone thrown by an invisible hand after this, caused a swelling and a soreness in her head; and she was bitten on both arms black and blue, and her breast scratched; the impression of the teeth, which were like a man's teeth, being seen by many.

"They deserted their house on these occasions, and though at a neighbor's house, they were at first haunted with apparitions, the satanical molestations quickly ceased. When Antonio returned unto his own house, at his entrance there, he heard one walking in his chamber, and saw the boards buckle under the feet of the walker; and yet there was nobody there. For this cause he went back to dwell on the other side of the river; but thinking he might plant his ground, though he left his house, he had five rods of good log fence thrown down at once, and the footing of neat cattle plainly to be seen almost between every row of corn in the field; yet no cattle seen there, nor any damage done to his corn, or so much as a leaf of it cropped."

A haunted house was pulled down at East Haven, Connecticut, during the necromantic period. Nothing very sinister or wicked occurred at this house, but people were alarmed by the sounds of revelry which came from the place at night. As there was then practically no night life in New England, it is easy to understand how startled the people of a quiet town would be to see a place they thought untenanted lit up, to say nothing of hearing the sound of ghostly hoofers inside wagging a merry toe. One would like to know what tunes the happy and harmless ghosts of East Haven danced to, but the account does not go beyond the few facts of the following paragraph.

"In an old lonely house which stood on the road leading to New Haven, lights were seen in the night; the sound of the violin, and the noise of persons dancing, was heard by the inhabitants of the places around it, until they went to work day after day, pulling its clapboards off, until the house was completely destroyed, to the joy of the inhabitants of the town."

John Greenleaf Whittier, writing on "The Supernaturalism of New England" in the *Democratic*

Review for 1843, speaks of a similar case near his house in the Merrimac Valley. "A former neighbor of mine,—a simple, honest mechanic,—used to amuse us by his reiterated complaints of the diabolical revels of certain evil spirits, which had chosen his garret for their ballroom. All night long he could hear a dance going on above him, regulated by some infernal melody. He had no doubt whatever of the supernatural character of the annoyance, and treated with contempt the suggestion of his neighbors, that, after all, it might be nothing more than the rats among his corn."

Some time after the disquieting manifestations in East Haven, the town of Granby, Connecticut, became notorious as the scene of unusual demonstrations. It is a noticeable fact that when one person in a place experienced something strange, other persons in the same town were apt to have similar experiences, until at length the place acquired quite a reputation as a theater of extraordinary events. Some families in Granby acted as if they were bewitched. They ran about in the craziest manner and said that they heard strange noises and saw spirits in the air. A whole company of ghosts seems to have played upon the fears of the people by rioting uncontrolled through the town.

Most puzzling of all were the activities of a juvenile ghost, which haunted a certain house on the outskirts of the town. Barber, who seems to be a major source of information for these supernatural happenings, says:

"About ten or twelve years since, in the west part of the town, in an old house near the Hartland line, the crying of a child, and many other unusual noises, were many times distinctly heard by persons who were in the house, although there was no child near, nor was there any apparent cause for any noise to be heard in the vicinity. Sometimes the crying of the child was very loud and distinct, and appeared to be but a few feet from the persons who heard it. It ought to be mentioned that in this house a foul crime is supposed to have been perpetrated. Two young men who were possessed of the usual share of courage, supposing the whole to be a kind of 'ghost story,' determined to sleep all night in the room where these noises were heard, and find out, if possible, the cause. Some time after they had gone to bed, in the dead of the night, something appeared to come with a kind of gust against the house, then something appeared to rush through the window, although nothing was seen; next the chairs were thrown about in great disorder, next there was a noise heard at the fireplace with the shovel and tongs, although there was none in the room, and finally the noise appeared to go off down the ash hole."

There was never any satisfactory explanation as to what it was that caused the commotion and then disappeared down the hole of the fireplace. Perhaps as good a solution as any was that offered by Samuel G. Goodrich, who seems to have read the foregoing account. "What could it have been," he said, "but Old Sooty himself?"

Singular as were the uncanny events at Granby, people marveled even more at the mysterious happenings at Sheffield, Massachusetts, just over the state line from Salisbury, Connecticut. Part of these occurrences took place in the former town and part in the latter. Once more we are indebted to Barber for the facts. He obtained them from members of the Sage family, who in 1836 were still living on the spot, and could then have been corroborated by a great number of living people. It is a moot point if human tricksters had a hand in this strange affair, or if it was the work of poltergeists, the noisy and malicious spirits of the invisible world. Whatever the answer, it was a curious business, as the Sage narration shows, and more knowledge, one way or the other, we are not likely to have at this distance of time.

"These occurrences commenced Nov. 8th, 1802,

at a clothier's shop. A man and two boys were in the shop; the boys had retired to rest, it being between 10 and 11 o'clock at night. A block of wood was thrown through the window; after that, pieces of hard mortar, till the man and boys became alarmed, and went to the house to call Mr. Sage, who arose from bed and went to the shop, and could hear the glass break often, but could not discover from whence it came, notwithstanding the night was very light. He exerted himself to discover the cause without success. It continued constantly till daylight, and then ceased till the next evening at 8 o'clock, when it commenced again, and continued till midnight; then ceased till the next evening at dusk, and continued till some time in the evening, and then ceased. The next day it commenced about an hour before sundown, and continued about an hour, and then it left the shop and began at the dwelling-house of Mr. Ezekiel Landon, 100 rods north in the town of Sheffield. It continued several hours, and ceased till the next morning; when the family were at breakfast it began again, and continued two or three hours, and ceased till evening, when it began again and continued several hours, and ceased till the next morning, when it began again and continued all the forenoon, and then ceased altogether. The articles thrown into the shop were pieces of wood, charcoal, stone, but principally pieces of hard mortar, such as could not be found in the neighborhood. Nothing but stones were thrown into the house of Mr. Landon, the first of which was thrown into the door. There were 38 panes of glass broke out of the shop, and 18 out of the dwelling houses: in two or three instances persons were hit by the things that were thrown. What was remarkable, nothing could be seen coming till the glass broke, and whatever passed through, fell directly down on the window-sill, as if it had been put through with a person's fingers, and many pieces of mortar and coal were thrown through the same hole in the glass in succession. Many hundreds of people assembled to witness the scene, among whom were clergymen and other gentlemen, but none were able to detect the source of the mischief. The more credulous readily believed it to be witchcraft, but it was generally thought to be some slight of hand, affected by a combination of individuals, as the windows were broken on different sides of the buildings at nearly the same time."

And here, perhaps, is as good a place as any to mention a deeply mysterious occurrence a few miles from Sheffield at Great Barrington. It is a traveler's tale picked up by Timothy Dwight. He said it was told to him by a respectable man, and he saw no reason to question the truth of the recital, except what is furnished by the nature of the story itself.

"A Mr. Van Rennselaer, a young gentleman from Albany, came one evening into an inn, kept by a Mr. Root, just at the eastern end of the bridge, which crosses the Hooestennuc in this town. The innkeeper, who knew him, asked him where he had crossed the river. He answered, 'On the bridge.' Mr. Root replied, that that was impossible, because it had been raised that very day, and that not a plank had been laid on it. Mr. Van Rennselaer said, that this could not be true; because his horse had come over without any difficulty or reluctance; that the night was indeed so profoundly dark, as to prevent him from seeing anything distinctly; but that it was incredible, if his horse could see sufficiently well to keep his footing anywhere, that he should not discern the danger, and impossible for him to pass over the bridge in that condition. Each went to bed dissatisfied, neither believing the story of the other. In the morning Mr. Van Rennselaer went, at the solicitation of his host, to view the bridge; and, finding it a naked frame, gazed for a moment with astonishment, and fainted."

Lest it be thought that all our hauntings occurred long ago, here is a modern instance from the *Boston Post* of no remoter date than August 20, 1941, when visitors were reported flocking to the old house in Henniker, New Hampshire, said to be haunted by the ghost of Ocean Born Mary. The name recalls one of the most interesting legends of old New England. With the kind permission of Mr. Richard Grozier, editor and publisher of the *Post*, the story is presented here in full.

"The Ocean Born Mary House has many visitors these late summer days," says the *Post* narrator "and vacationists are finding their way up in the hills and saving gasoline by leaving their cars in the big field at the foot of the long hill and walking up the dusty road that leads to the red house.

"The story of Ocean Born Mary is a familiar legend to residents of Henniker. In the early eighteenth century, a child was born on a sailing vessel headed for this country from Scotland. A pirate chief boarded the vessel in mid-ocean and was prepared to massacre the crew and passengers when noticing the three-day-old infant, he took the baby in his arms and ran about the ship, shouting:

" 'In the name of my sainted mother, I christen thee Ocean Born Mary; live long, child, and may you prosper.'

"A few minutes later, he left the ship with his crew to return in a boat with two bolts of figured blue silk, saying to the parents of the child: 'Le

Mary wear this for her wedding dress when she becomes a bride.'

"Tradition has it that he released his prisoners and allowed them to continue their voyage to this country. Ocean Born Mary came to Henniker in 1780, built the house which now bears her name, and died here in 1814. A monument can be seen today in the little cemetery at the foot of the hill.

"Back in 1937, students of psychic phenomena and descendants of Ocean Born Mary, acting on reports that the woman's spirit still walked, obtained a piece of the original silk from which the wedding dress was made, and returned to the house to observe the 215th anniversary of her birth.

"Eagerly the little group awaited for some sign of recognition from the spirit world, but nothing was manifested at the time, for, according to one medium present, a condition was prevalent that could not be righted, and other meetings were planned for a later date.

"Gus Roy, the present owner of the house, who came here several years ago from a Western city, firmly believes that Ocean Born Mary's spirit still haunts the old home, and his mother is certain that she has been in close touch with her, not once, but many times.

"When the Roys first came to the house, doors fastened securely at night were found wide open in the morning, and often in the still of night voices could be heard, it was said. Other manifestations have also been made, it was said, and visitors enjoyed visiting the place.

"Some come here as investigators and others share the belief of the mother and son who have lived here for several years. Mr. Roy believes pirate gold, pieces of doubloon and eight are buried somewhere about the 100-acre tract of land. In fact, he has dug up the cellar and now plans to move the big hearthstone in the kitchen in an effort to find the buried treasure."

A better known New Hampshire legend is that of General Jonathan Moulton of Hampton, the Yankee Faust, who is supposed to have sold himself to the Devil in consideration of the latter periodically filling his boots with gold and silver. The general, who was an avaricious man, procured the largest pair of jack boots he could find and stood them in the fireplace, where the Devil could pour the money down the chimney directly into them. Then the canny Moulton thought of a way to cheat the Devil. He cut the toes out of the boots, so that when the Devil poured the cash down the chimney it rolled out on the floor of the room. When the Devil found he had been tricked, he is said to have burned the house down in revenge; but the place still stands and is pointed to as a famous haunted establishment. Readers who always think of the Devil as a tall, dark, and handsome man, dressed in doublet and scarlet tights, will be disappointed to learn that when he visited the miserly general and made his compact with him he was dressed in a black velvet suit.

"When the general died," says Whittier, "he was laid out and placed in a coffin as usual; but on the day of the funeral it was whispered about that his body was missing, and the neighbors came to the charitable conclusion that the enemy had got his own at last."

Whittier's bedroom ballad, "The New Wife and the Old," is based on another legend to the effect that, when General Moulton's first wife died under suspicious circumstances, the aging warrior wooed and won a young woman who had been his dead wife's friend. According to the poet, it was a case of

> Blooming girl and manhood gray
> Autumn in the arms of May!

On their wedding night the second Mrs. Moulton felt a cold hand take from her finger the ring which had belonged to the first wife. Her shrieks of fear awakened her husband. Search was made for the ring, but it was never found.

For many years the ghosts of General Moulton and his wife disturbed the inmates of the mansion, the bewigged general in a snuff-colored suit tapping about the house with a gold-headed cane and her dress "a-rustling up and down the stairs." At last, to allay the fears of the servants, a minister was called in to exorcise the ghosts. This was done in the presence of many Hampton people. The ceremony of laying the ghosts was apparently successful, as there were no more complaints about either the general or his wife.

The summit of ghostly happenings in New England was reached at Stratford, Connecticut, on Sunday morning March 10, 1850, when the Rev. Eliakim Phelps, D.D., returning home from church, was astonished to find the front door of his home hung with crepe. Disconcerting and dismal as was this discovery, it was nothing to what he found inside. For laid out in the best room was a human figure swathed for burial. Naturally, the finding of the crepe on the door and the phantom corpse within upset the Sunday calm of the Phelps's home. No less, it shattered the peace of the rest of the town, which seethed with excitement for weeks as other amazing conjurations followed.

Spiritualism was just beginning to sweep the country, and as news of the strange affair at Stratford-on-Housatonic spread, clouds of pressmen, spiritualists, and other investigators descended on the town. Swarms of curiosity seekers, necromancy hunters, professional ghost layers, scoffing confuters, and other unquenchable fools were to be seen hanging about the place at all hours of the day and night. Especially joyful were the penny-a-liners and romanticists of the press, one of whom, an unprincipled fellow from Bridgeport, strolling shamelessly beyond the bounds of truth, invented an Arabian Nights' tale about a scissors-grinder who stopped before the house and suddenly, in plain view of several persons, began to ascend into the air. He went up and up, turning his wheels steadily all the while, until at length he was lost to view, like the person in the Indian rope trick. It was said that he came down the next day in Waterbury. A rival paper promptly branded the story as a low and malicious falsehood.

Interest is lent to this case by the fact that the haunted house still stands in Stratford, where after more than a century of existence it remains one of the town's finest residences. It was built during the Greek revival period and has a porticoed front with four large Doric columns. But its most remarkable architectural feature is inside. This is the great ground floor hallway extending through the house, with its twin staircases, one rising from the front door, the other from the rear door. The house was built for a sea captain in the China trade whose wife, in planning the mansion, insisted that the hall should be the same length as the ship's deck which her husband was used to pacing, namely, seventy feet; and the twin staircases, meeting at a spacious common landing, were provided to create for the captain the illusion of mounting by one flight of stairs to the hurricane deck of his ship and descending by the other to the main deck.

Exterior and interior views of the house may be seen in William Howard Wilcoxson's interesting *History of Stratford* (1940), to which I am indebted for the facts of the haunting and the contemporary press reports of the case. The house, it must be said, does not live up to the usual academic picture of a haunted place. There is nothing dark or sinister about it. Mushrooms do not sprout between the stone flagging in the basement kitchen. When I asked some people who know the present owner and have slept in the house more than once if anything went bump in the night, they were surprised to learn that anything unusual had ever transpired there. They had never heard of the case of the so-called Stratford Knockings.

All sorts of alarming things happened in the house. Apparitions were seen and strange sounds were heard echoing through the halls. There were not only mysterious rappings on beds and doors but prodigious thwacks, which seemed to make the house as well as the inmates quake with fear. No one was hurt, but there were many narrow escapes from flying bric-a-brac and furniture. The property damage was considerable. And things grew worse instead of better. More than a month after the fateful Sunday this item appeared in a Connecticut newspaper:

"The carryings on at the house of Rev. Mr. Phelps in Stratford, are becoming more and more dreadful. The furniture of the house becomes occasionally bewitched, and knocks itself to pieces and the deuce is to pay with the children's clothing. One of the enquiring visitants was sitting with the family the other evening, when an earthenware pitcher got up from the table and flew at a young lady of the family, and just missing her went ker-smash against the side of the room. The visitor thinking the young lady unusually attractive took her by the hand, when, he says, he received an electric shock."

Newspaper editors, not content with sending their reporters, visited the much-haunted house themselves, talked with members of the family, and watched for developments in the hope of shedding light on the mystery. In most cases, they arrived as skeptics and departed unconvinced that supernatural forces were at work in the house. Yet they were unable to solve the mystery. They failed to find any person masquerading in astral gray or any spirit trailing clouds of ectoplasm. Baffled in their probings, they fell back on the explanation that nothing that occurred was of such a character as to exclude absolutely the human element.

During the visit of the editor of the Bridgeport *Standard*, over two months after the first manifestation, the haunters of the house were still active, for we find the editor writing:

"Owing perhaps to our skepticism, the demonstrations on this occasion were not very wonderful, although one of the trio was of a different opinion. One chair was upset—a large rocking chair was carried across the room and dashed against the door, and the drawer of a bureau was taken from its place and thrown upon the floor with a thundering noise. These occurrences took place in the sleeping room of the young lady who has been (and perhaps unjustly) accused of playing upon the credulity of the public. The room is connected by a door with another chamber used as a lodging room by the family, and the door on this occasion was open. The demonstrations came on after eleven o'clock, just after the family had retired. The watchers were in the hall near the door of the young lady's room, or were in the front chambers. On hearing the chair upset, they, as usual on such occasions, rushed into the room, and there was the chair on the floor! After expressing their wonder etc., they retired. After a while the rocking chair went through its performance, and made a decided dent in the door. It lay, in fact, against the door, as we attempted to get in, and the young lady said it passed over the bed where she was lying. After the watchers had retired, the drawer, half full of various articles, sprang out of the bureau and cut up its didos—no one, of course, being in the room but the young lady and to all appearances she had not moved. It will, of course, occur to everyone, that if so disposed she might have done all these strange things and returned to bed before the door was opened. One of the watchers, after pretending to walk away with the others, returned as quietly as possible after the door had been closed, in order to open it on the instant in case there was any further noise, but for the rest of the night the house was as still as a church—and this is all we know of the Stratford Knockings.

"We do not believe that Dr. Phelps, and his lady, were parties to any deception, nor have we any special reasons for intimating that the lady is carrying on a hoax for her own amusement. We don't feel disposed to make such a charge, but the facts, as far as we could observe, were precisely as stated. We ought perhaps in fairness to add that when several ladies spent the night in the room with her the carryings on were much more remarkable than on this occasion. The family is a very respectable one, and all the members seem to be very much distressed by the doings. Out of the statements that have been made the public will draw their own conclusion."

This account evidently drew the fire of another Connecticut editor, because a few days later the *Standard* felt obliged to explain its position.

"Our friend of the Waterbury *American* seems to consider us almost a convert in the matter of the Stratford manifestations, or, in all events, somewhat noncommittal. We are as skeptical as ever, we have neither seen nor heard anything which induces a belief that spirit agencies are, or ever believe were at work, in the haunted house. At the same time we do not feel disposed to regard as fools all those who happen to think differently, nor are we disposed to charge the family, or heads of it, with hoax. The house is so constructed that mischievous inmates or neighbors, can easily play a variety of tricks with least risk of detection. So it seems to us. We suggested this to Dr. Phelps and he remarked that such was his own opinion until he was compelled to believe otherwise. We are under no such compulsion, and the evidence, so far as we know, is altogether insufficient to warrant the conclusion drawn by some of the neighbors. In short, we take all these, Rochester, Newark and Stratford Doings to be the work of humbug in some form or shape, but we do not know that this is the case, and are willing to hear all that can be heard on the other side and to receive all the evidence with a fair valuation."

The editor of the New Haven *Journal* and the editor of the New Haven *Palladium* were among those who took the processional route to Stratford. Of their experiences there the former wrote:

"Shortly after our introduction to the family, the boy, a lad of nearly fourteen, went out of the room and soon one of the ladies of the house came running in, exclaiming that Henry was gone, and couldn't be found. A general scream followed by general rush of men and women, young and old, clergymen and lawyers, editors, loafers, etc., made a rush to the back of the house, one to one place, and another to another, helter skelter, hurry skurry, for him till the boy was found under the hay against the side of the barn, and when pulled out, he assumed a sleepy look. Eyes heavy shut, as though in a comatose state, together with the loss of consciousness and voluntary motion. We pitied the father, who seemed distressed by the apprehension of his son being strangled, as on a former occasion he had been found with a rope around his neck perched up on a shelf in a closet. After nearly an hour of apparent stupidity the boy came out of his lethargic state, and when questioned, said he was flying his kite in the yard, and the next he knew he was in the barn."

The editor of the *Palladium* had this to say of the work of the poltergeists:

"We were shown the broken candlestick, the broken pitcher, some thirty or forty broken panes of glass in the windows, the bruised bedstead, etc. —all of which appearance showed a bold persevering and very destructive disposition on the part of somebody or something—how skillfully all this destruction was accomplished, we cannot say, not having witnessed any of it. . . . We readily grant that the worthy gentleman of the house is perfectly sincere in his own opinion in regard to the matter. But that his views are founded in error we are forced to believe, both from the absence of any demonstration in our presence to the contrary, and also from their variance with the known laws of nature and Providence, and with the history of mankind."

Everybody at the time, even the most incredulous, joined in giving Dr. Phelps a clean bill of health. Opinion was unanimous that he was not attempting to hoodwink the public in any way. His integrity and intelligence, indeed, constituted an important element in the case, lending strength to the belief of many that the ghostly presences in the Phelps home were genuine. For how could such a man, it was reasoned, be deluded? Nowhere is to be found the slightest hint that he knew more than he chose to tell, or that he had any inkling as to the person or persons, if any, responsible for the outrageous and sensational occurrences in his home. Throughout the whole affair Dr. Phelps gives the impression of a candid and sincere man of physical and moral courage for whom the perplexing and hair-raising events were a great trial. Writing in the New York *Observer* of the strange happenings, particularly the messages rapped out by the visiting spirits, the harassed clergyman said:

"For days and weeks together I have watched these strange movements with all the care and caution and close attention which I can bestow. I witnessed them hundreds and hundreds of times, and I know that in hundreds of instances they took place when there was no visible power by which the motion could have been produced. Scores of persons, of standing in the community, whose education, general intelligence, candor, veracity and sound judgment were without question, were requested to witness the phenomena, and, if possible, help us to a solution of the mystery but as yet no such solution has been attained. The idea that the whole was a 'trick of the children'—an idea which some of the papers have endeavored with great zeal to promulgate as to everyone acquainted with the fact—is as false as it is injurious.

"About the middle of April, a gentleman who was spending a night at my house, purposed to try a method of interrogation which had been adopted in western New York and to our utter amusement a series of responses were returned. From each, the inference was irresistible that they must have been produced by a being which possessed intelligence. For several weeks, communications were made in the way of relating most wholly to a matter which certain members of the family are supposed to have an interest; at the same time the other manifestations continued, and very great annoyance was experienced. The mode of communication was by some person repeating the alphabet and the letters of the word to be uttered were indicated by a rap from some invisible agent. I tried by all methods I could devise to find what the power was by which the rapping was produced. I have heard it hundreds of times, and have done my best to ascertain the cause, but as yet I have not succeeded. I have been often asked if I believe it was the work of spirits. I have as often replied that I do not know what it is. I have never seen the spirit and I do not know what a spirit could do if it would or what it would do if it could. The facts, however, are of such a nature and have transpired under such circumstances as to render the idea a trick or design deception wholly inadmissible. Still, however, I have become fully satisfied that no reliance whatever is to be placed on these communications, either as a source of valuable information or as a means of acquiring truth. I speak of what has transpired at my house and I have the fullest confidence, that if it is the work of spirits, it is the work of wicked spirits.

"Indeed, they profess to be wicked spirits in a state of torment seeking mitigation of their torment by redressing the wrongs of which they were guilty in life. I have watched the progress of this matter with great care, and have done the best in my power to learn what these strange things mean; and although I have not yet been able to ascertain the cause I am satisfied their communications are wholly worthless. They are often contradictory—often proved false, frequently trifling and nonsensical, and more in character with what might be expected from loafers on a spree, than what might be expected from spirits returned from the world of retribution, to tell the secrets of their prison house."

The New York *Independent* did not believe that there had been any meeting of the visible and invisible worlds at Stratford, and in support of this hypothesis printed this report:

"A gentleman who has visited the scenes of the Stratford Development reports, among the mvsteries, of the following:

"1. The servant girl, who was supposed to be gone to Bridgeport to church when the first display took place continues to reside contentedly in the house haunted by evil spirits, without even calling the Priest.

"2. After the Rochester Book was procured and studied by the inmates of the house the spirit became capable of communicating information by knocking 'but the information was only on subjects known to the family.'

"3. Several sober and worthy people of good education, supposed that these occurrences 'which are all of a kind' easily produced by human agencies must be supernatural, because they did not see anybody do it when they are not looking. No one has seen that they began to move without human agency.

"4. A distinguished Presbyterian clergyman has been deluded in his old age by his zealous devotion to mesmerism, and particularly by the tricks of some about him, to take a journey to Philadelphia to investigate certain claims on the testimony of the concealed author of the knockings."

Mr. Wilcoxson, the Stratford historian, says incredulous Stratfordians at last found an explanation of the mystery in the middle-aged clergyman's young wife. Accustomed to the gay life of the city and becoming bored with the quieter amenities of life in Stratford, she chose the extraordinary means recited to effect a change. In this, it is said, she was aided by her two clever children, the girl and boy mentioned in the despatches from Stratford. If this is the correct solution, the hoaxers succeeded, at least as far as affecting their deliverance from Stratford was concerned, as shortly after the family moved away. Coincidentally, the activities of the poltergeists ceased, and no one who has since lived in the house has been disturbed by them in any way. Perhaps some day the inside story of the haunting will be disclosed, but not yet, apparently, is the "due time" when this amazing affair shall be "revealed and brought to light."

TO BEHOLD PHANTOM SHIPS

WHILE New England may not be so well stocked with haunted houses as might be wished, it has a fair number of ghost ships. Connecticut, Rhode Island, and Maine each has its legend of a specter vessel. These legends attracted the nineteenth-century New England poets, who found the writing of ballads based on the folklore of the region a pleasant and profitable line of trade. It was inevitable that in casting about for material they should run afoul the phantom ships; inevitable, too, that they should celebrate them in verse.

William Cullen Bryant wanted to write about the Phantom Ship of New Haven but, learning that Washington Irving had made some use of the legend, gave up the idea, only to have Longfellow step in and exploit it. It is one of the earliest and best of the New England maritime legends. Authority for it rests on a letter written by the Rev. James Pierpont of New Haven to Cotton Mather of Boston, who included it in his *Magnalia Christi*. Mather is often treated as a figure of comedy, a stuffy, pedantic fellow, but the old colonial deserves our gratitude for his curiosity and industry in collecting and preserving from oblivion many facts of great historic interest. Among the things which interested him was the strange phenomenon of the Phantom Ship of New Haven. Accordingly, he wrote to Mr. Pierpont in New Haven, from whom he received this reply.

"*Reverend and Dear Sir*—

"In compliance with your desires, I now give you the relation of that *apparition* of a *ship in the air*, which I have received from the most credible, judicious and curious surviving observers of it.

"In the year 1647, besides much other lading, a

far more rich treasure of passengers, (five or six of which were persons of chief note and worth in New Haven,) put themselves on board a new ship, built at Rhode Island, of about 150 tuns; but so walty, that the master (Lamberton) often said she would prove their grave. In the month of January, cutting their way through much ice, on which they were accompanied with Reverend Mr. Davenport, besides many other friends, with many fears, as well as prayers and tears, they set sail. Mr. Davenport, in prayer, with an observable emphasis, used these words: *Lord, if it be thy pleasure to bury these our friends in the bottom of the sea, they are thine; save them!* The spring following, no tidings of these friends arrived with the ships from England: New Haven's heart began to fail her: This put the godly people on much prayer, both public and private, *that the Lord would (if it was his pleasure) let them hear what he had done with their dear friends, and prepare them with a suitable submission to his Holy Will.* In June next ensuing, a great thunder storm broke out of the northwest; after which (the hemisphere being serene), about an hour before sun-set, a ship of like dimensions with the aforesaid, with her canvass and colours abroad, (though the wind northernly,) appeared in the air coming up from our harbour's mouth, which lyes southward from the town, seemingly with her sails filled under a fresh gale, holding her course north, and continuing under observation, sailing against the wind for the space of half an hour.

"Many were drawn to behold this great work of God; yea, the very children cryed out, *There's a brave ship!* At length crouding up as far as there is usually water sufficient for such a vessel, and so near some of the spectators, as that they imagined a man might hurl a stone on board her, her maintop seemed to be blown off, but left hanging in the shrouds; then her missen-top; then all her masting seemed blown away by the board: quickly after the hulk brought unto a careen, she overset, and so vanished into a smoaky cloud, which in some time dissipated, leaving, as every where else, a clear air. The admiring spectators could distinguish the several colours of each part, the principal rigging, and such proportions, as caused not only the generality of persons to say, *This was the mould of their ship, and this was her tragick end:* but Mr. Davenport also in publick declared to this effect: *That God had condescended, for the quieting of their afflicted spirits, this extraordinary account of his sovereign disposal of those for whom so many fervent prayers were made continually.*

"Thus I am, Sir, your humble servant,

"James Pierpont."

Not much is known of this amazing occurrence beyond what is contained in the letter. The loss was a grievous blow to New Haven. As a result of trade disappointments, the colonists had pooled almost the last of their resources and put them into the vessel and her cargo, in the hope of recouping their fortunes. They thought New Haven unsuited to agriculture, and when the Phantom Ship appeared to confirm their worst fears as to the fate of their argosy, they began to plan the abandonment of the colony and their return to the Old World. Negotiations were carried on for a place to settle in Galloway, but after long delays these broke down, and eventually the colonists rid themselves of the notion that they could not succeed as husbandmen. "Their posterity," says an old account, "who they thought would be reduced to beggary, made respectable farmers, and flourished no less than their neighbors."

One repercussion of the tragedy that was felt in the neighboring colony of Hartford was the loss of the manuscript of a book written by the Rev. Thomas Hooker, who had the misfortune to dispatch his work to a London publisher by the ill-fated vessel.

In 1857, when he was fifty years old, Longfellow turned the facts of Pierpont's report into the following poem:

THE PHANTOM SHIP

In Mather's Magnalia Christi,
  Of the old colonial time,
May be found in prose the legend
  That is here set down in rhyme.

A ship sailed from New Haven,
  And the keen and frosty airs,
That filled her sails at parting,
  Were heavy with good men's prayers.

"O Lord! if it be thy pleasure"—
  Thus prayed the old divine—
"To bury our friends in the ocean,
  Take them, for they are thine!"

But Master Lamberton muttered,
  And under his breath said he,
"This ship is so crank and walty,
  I fear our grave she will be!"

And the ships that came from England,
  When the winter months were gone,
Brought no tidings of this vessel
  Nor of Master Lamberton.

This put the people to praying
  That the Lord would let them hear
What in his greater wisdom
  He had done with friends so dear.

And at last their prayers were answered:
  It was in the month of June,
An hour before the sunset
  Of a windy afternoon,

When steadily stearing landward,
  A ship was seen below,
And they knew it was Lamberton, Master,
  Who sailed so long ago.

On she came, with a cloud of canvas,
  Right against the wind that blew,
Until the eye could distinguish
  The faces of the crew.

Then fell the straining topmasts,
  Hanging in the shrouds,
And her sails were loosened and lifted,
  And blown away like clouds.

And the masts, with all their rigging,
  Fell slowly, one by one,
And the bulk dilated and vanished,
  As a sea-mist in the sun!

And the people who saw this marvel
  Each said unto his friend,
That this was the mould of their vessel,
  And thus her tragic end.

And the pastor of the village
  Gave thanks to God in prayer,
That, to quiet their troubled spirits,
  He had sent this Ship of Air.

If the poet Bryant regretted his abandonment of the Connecticut ghost ship and its subsequent seizure by Longfellow, he may have felt some satisfaction when Whittier invaded Maine and, taking a similar seacoast legend from the shores of Longfellow's own Casco Bay, wrote, in "The Dead Ship of Harpswell," a better poem than "The Phantom Ship." If Longfellow was inclined to consider Whittier a carpetbagger for taking this Maine material, he was in no position to complain, since he himself felt free to roam at large in quest of themes. The surprising thing is that he should have overlooked such good material lying in his own front yard, so to speak.

Asked for the source of his information, Whittier said, "Some twenty years ago I received from Miss Marion Pearl, daughter of Rev. Mr. Pearl, a well known clergyman of Maine, a letter, descriptive of the people, habits, superstitions, and legends of Orr's Island, where, I think, the writer was a teacher. The legend of a spectre ship, as described in my poem, interested me by its weird suggestiveness. I have no doubt that a quarter of a century ago the legend was talked of on the island by the aged people. Perhaps it has died out now. The school teacher has been abroad since, and the new generation are ashamed of the fireside lore of their grandmothers."

Orr's Island is, of course, the scene of Harriet Beecher Stowe's romance, *The Pearl of Orr's Island*. Close by is Ragged Island, which is owned by Edna St. Vincent Millay. Whittier wrote his traditional poem of this region in 1866.

THE DEAD SHIP OF HARPSWELL

What flecks the outer gray beyond
  The sundown's golden trail?
The white flash of a sea-bird's wing,
  Or gleam of slanting sail?
Let young eyes watch from Neck and Point,
  And sea-worn elders pray,—
The ghost of what was once a ship
  Is sailing up the bay!

To Behold Phantom Ships

From gray sea-fog, from icy drift,
  From peril and from pain,
The home-bound fisher greets thy lights,
  O hundred-harbored Maine!
But many a keel shall seaward turn,
  And many a sail outstand,
When, tall and white, the Dead Ship looms
  Against the dusk of land.

She rounds the headland's bristling pines;
  She threads the isle-set bay;
No spur of breeze can speed her on,
  Nor ebb of tide delay.
Old men still walk the Isle of Orr
  Who tell her date and name,
Old shipwrights sit in Freeport yards
  Who hewed her oaken frame.

What weary doom of baffled quest,
  Thou sad sea-ghost, is thine?
What makes thee in the haunts of home
  A wonder and a sign?
No foot is on thy silent deck,
  Upon thy helm no hand;
No ripple hath the soundless wind
  That smites thee from the land!

For never comes the ship to port,
  Howe'er the breeze may be;
Just when she nears the waiting shore
  She drifts again to sea.
No tack of sail, nor turn of helm,
  Nor sheer of veering side;
Stern-fore she drives to sea and night,
  Against the wind and tide.

In vain o'er Harpswell Neck the star
  Of evening guides her in;
In vain for her the lamps are lit
  Within thy tower, Seguin!
In vain the harbor-boat shall hail,
  In vain the pilot call;
No hand shall reef her spectral sail,
  Or let her anchor fall.

Shake, brown old wives, with dreary joy,
  Your gray-head hints of ill;
And, over sick-beds whispering low,
  Your prophecies fulfil.
Some home amid yon birchen trees
  Shall drape its door with woe;
And slowly where the Dead Ship sails,
  The burial boat shall row!

From Wolf Neck and from Flying Point,
From island and from main,
From sheltered cove and tided creek,
Shall glide the funeral train.
The dead-boat with the bearers four,
The mourners at her stern,—
And one shall go the silent way
Who shall no more return!

And men shall sigh, and women weep,
Whose dear ones pale and pine,
And sadly over sunset seas
Await the ghostly sign.
They know not that its sails are filled
By pity's tender breath,
Nor see the Angel at the helm
Who steers the ship of death!

The subject of ghost ships apparently fascinated Whittier, for the following year we find him writing of another phantom craft, "The Palatine," the story of which he summarizes in a headnote to the poem:

"Block Island in Long Island Sound, called by the Indians Manisees, the isle of the little god, was the scene of a tragic incident a hundred years or more ago, when *The Palatine*, an emigrant ship bound for Philadelphia, driven off its course, came upon the coast at this point. A mutiny on board, followed by an inhuman desertion on the part of the crew, had brought the unhappy passengers to the verge of starvation and madness. Tradition says that the wreckers on shore, after rescuing all but one of the survivors, set fire to the vessel, which was driven out to sea before the gale which had sprung up. Every twelvemonth, according to the same tradition, the spectacle of a ship on fire is visible to the inhabitants of the island."

The legend was told to Whittier by a Newport friend. There are various versions of the affair, which differ somewhat in detail, but in the main follow the general pattern as outlined by the poet. The specter was seen by dwellers on the mainland in the vicinity of Westerly, Rhode Island, as well as by watchers on the island. The best account of it is in the following letter written in 1811 by Dr. Aaron C. Willey of Block Island to Dr. Samuel Mitchell of New York.

"This curious irradiation rises from the ocean near the northern part of the island. Its appearance is nothing different from a blaze of fire. Whether it actually touches the water, or merely hovers over

t, is uncertain. . . . Sometimes it is small, re-
ɜembling the light through a distant window; at
ɔthers expanding to the highness of a ship with all
ıer canvas spread. . . . It is seen at all seasons of
he year, and for the most part in the calm weather
which precedes an easterly or southerly storm. . . .
ts continuance is sometimes but transient, and
ɔthers throughout the night. . . . The first time I
aw it, it was evening twilight, in February, 1810.
t was large and gently lambent, very bright,
ɔroad at the bottom, and terminating acutely up-
vard. . . . It continued about fifteen minutes
rom the time I first observed it. . . . This lucid
neteor has long been known as the Palatine Light.
3y the ignorant and superstitious it is thought to be
upernatural. Its appellation originated from that of
vessel called the *Palatine*, which was designedly
:ast away at this place in the beginning of the last
:entury, in order to conceal, as tradition reports,
nhuman treatment and murder of some of the un-
ortunate passengers. From this time, it is said, the
'alatine Light appeared; and there are many who
ɔelieve it to be a ship of fire, to which their fan-
astic imaginations figure masts, ropes, and flowing
ails."

Here, stripped of its outer wrappings, is the heart
f Whittier's poem:

THE PALATINE

Old wives spinning their webs of tow,
Or rocking weirdly to and fro
In and out of the peat's dull glow,

And old men mending their nets of twine,
Talk together of dream and sign,
Talk of the lost ship Palatine,—

The ship that, a hundred years before,
Freighted deep with its goodly store,
In the gales of the equinox went ashore.

The eager islanders one by one
Counted the shots of her signal gun,
And heard the crash when she drove right on!

Into the teeth of death she sped:
(May God forgive the hands that fed
The false lights over the rocky Head!)

O men and brothers! what sights were there!
White upturned faces, hands stretched in prayer
Where waves had pity, could ye not spare?

Down swooped the wreckers, like birds of prey
Tearing the heart of the ship away,
And the dead had never a word to say.

And then with ghastly shimmer and shine
Over the rocks and the seething brine,
They burned the wreck of the Palatine.

In their cruel hearts, as they homeward sped,
"The sea and the rocks are dumb," they said:
"There'll be no reckoning with the dead."

But the year went round, and when once more
Along their foam-white curves of shore
They heard the line-storm rave and roar,

Behold! again, with shimmer and shine,
Over the rocks and the seething brine,
The flaming wreck of the Palatine!

So, haply in fitter words than these,
Mending their nets on their patient knees,
They tell the legend of Manisees.

No explanation of this roving brightness was ever made, and it will probably always remain a mystery of the sea.

There were other instances of phantom ships being seen in New England. At Lynn, Massachusetts, in 1682, a man named Handford and his wife saw one in the western sky at twilight. The ship was a handsome, black-hulled craft, with white sails and a superb banner streaming from the top of her mainmast. She was under full sail and headed south but, although seemingly in motion, made no progress. Just before sighting the phantom ship, Mr. and Mrs. Handford saw a strange black cloud in the west in which was the figure of a man fully armed, standing with his feet apart and holding a pike across his breast. In this same cloud the ship later made its appearance. Many people besides the Handfords saw the apparition of the ship, which was as plainly visible as any vessel in their own harbor, and all agreed that it was a magnificent sight. Its appearance in the heavens seems to have had no connection with any earthly happenings.

In *An Account of Two Voyages to New England* (1674), John Josselyn mentions two ghost ships which he says were believed to have been produced by witches. One was a shallop seen at sea manned by women, and the other a ship in a small cove on the coast of Maine, with a great red horse standing by the mainmast, which "vanished of a suddain."

TO ADOPT PECULIAR PLACE NAMES

HENRY JAMES did not care for the traditional pattern of New England place names. He thought many of them failed to minister to the poetry of association. Charming places, charming objects, he declared, languished under designations that seemed to leave on them the smudge of a vulgar thumb. Places suffering beneath some familiar, tasteless infliction of a name also appeared to turn up to him the plaintive eye of a creature wounded with a poisoned arrow. Nor was his dislike of these names confined to New England. He found them a source of irritation throughout the American scene.

Whether one agrees with him or not, it is certain that even the crudest and cruelest names often possess historic value, as when they preserve old descriptions, or commemorate bygone events and persons worth remembering, or are indicative of the origin of the early settlers, or the political and religious faiths which they held. Much of a region's history may be learned by studying its toponymy.

Samuel G. Goodrich, who won fame and fortune writing children's books under the pseudonym of Peter Parley, gives an illustration of this when he says of Woodbury, Connecticut, "Its names trace out its story. Quassapaug Lake, Shepaug River, Quanopaug Falls, Nonnewaug Falls, tell us of its original proprietors: Rattlesnake Rock, and White Deer Hills, bespeak the ancient inhabitants of the forest: Bethel Rock, Carmel Hill, and Tophet Hollow, announce the arrival here of the Pilgrim settlers from New Haven: Hall's Rock, Good Hill, Lightning's Playground, Scuppo, Hazel Plain, Moose Horn Hill, Ash Swamp, all in Woodbury or the vicinity, indicate alike certain traits of scenery, with the final settlement of the country by the English."

James Russell Lowell liked the homely, country

names of New England. In one of his native poems he mentions a mountain called Great Haystack and then goes on to say:

> I love these names,
> Wherewith the lonely farmer tames
> Nature to mute companionship
> With his own mind's domestic mood,
> And strives the surly world to clip
> In the arms of familiar habitude.

But there is reason to believe that Oliver Wendell Holmes shared to some extent Henry James's dislike of our nomenclature, because many place names are personal, and of personal names he remarked at the breakfast table, "Was there ever anything like the Yankee for inventing the most uncouth, pretentious, and detestable appellations,—inventing or finding them,—since the days of Praise-God Barebones? How can a man name an innocent new-born child, that never did any harm, Hiram?"

There is in Maine a town called Hiram, which an early settler christened in its nascency after Hiram, King of Tyre.

It would require a very large book indeed to cover adequately the subject of New England territorial names. Research would have to be carried on abroad, as many New England places were customarily named after the home towns in England of leading colonial settlers, many of these names going back many centuries, sometimes to a period long before the discovery of America. But investigating their original significance would have something of the fascination of reading a good detective story.

An example of the interesting character of the history revealed in tracing the origin of these transplanted names is found in the case of Litchfield, Connecticut, which was named after the English midland town of Lichfield, whose spires are familiar to thousands of American tourists who have seen them on their way up to London from Liverpool. This Staffordshire town was the birthplace of Dr. Johnson, whose father had a bookshop there, wherein the youthful Samuel worked when he wasn't too busy reading to the neglect of customers. The name is made up of the Anglo-Saxon word "lic," a corpse or body, and the word "field," the combination meaning field of corpses. Lichfield commemorates the traditional slaughter of a thousand Christians who are said to have suffered martyrdom there during the time of Diocletian.

The word "lic," it is interesting to note in passing, is also found in lich gate, the gate to a churchyard where the body was rested when being borne into the yard for burial. Modern lich gates are to be seen in New England, but are seldom designed to serve their original purpose. They are usually erected as garden entrances, or to mark the approaches to houses, and, though not unpicturesque, are apt to give one familiar with their origin a historic chill.

Differences in spelling between the same American and English place names are common. Thus in the case of the New England town of Litchfield just cited, there is an extra letter, an excrescent *t*, not found in the parent name. Corruptions and assimilations of this kind occurred in a variety of ways. Sometimes it was the result of carelessness or ignorance or poor calligraphy in drawing the original petition to the colonial assembly or general court, or it may have occurred from these or other causes when the resolution bestowing the name was drafted. Certainly the results were occasionally surprising, as when the people of Kenilworth, Connecticut, awoke to find that their town had been legally dubbed Killingworth. The person who drew the petition must have been all but illiterate, or else his handwriting resembled a dance of drunken beetles. But the name stuck, as has also that of another Connecticut town, Willington, which it was intended should be called Wellington, after the Somersetshire town of that name, whence later the Duke of Wellington derived his title. Misspelling was likewise responsible for the present name of a Maine town, Orrington, which the people wanted christened Orangetown.

An error in spelling, a single wrong letter in its name, cost the town of Littleton, Massachusetts, a fine bell. When the place was incorporated in 1715, it was called Littleton after the Hon. George Lyttleton, Esq., a member of Parliament, and one of the commissioners of the Treasury. In acknowledgment of the honor, this gentleman presented the town with a church bell; but because the *i* was inadvertently substituted for the *y* in the name, the gift miscarried, and was finally withheld, "under the pretense that no such town as Lyttleton, to which the bell was to be presented, could anywhere be found." More than a century later the bell was said to be still in use by the Massachusetts town which bought it.

Pronunciation, too, has played a part in these changes, some of which were made deliberately. Hartford, Connecticut, for example, was named after Hertford, a case of spelling the English name as it was pronounced. This was not only a harmless change which in no way altered the original meaning but was even an improvement, since the name is a pun, like Oxford, meaning ford of harts. Hartford and Hertford are both river towns. In similar manner, Barkhampstead, Connecticut, was named after Berkhampstead in Hertfordshire.

Pronunciation, or rather mispronunciation, led the people of Beverly, Massachusetts, to ask that the name of the town be changed to Budleigh. The reasons for the change are set forth in the quaint petition of Roger Conant, who made the request in 1671.

"Now my umble sute and request is unto this honorable Court onlie that the name of our town or plantation may be altered or changed from Beverly, and be called Budleigh. I have two reasons that have moved me unto this request: the first is, the great dislike and discontent of many of our people for this name Beverly, because (wee being but a small place) it hath caused us the constant nickname of beggarly, being in the mouths of many, and no order was given, or consent by the people, to their agent, for any name until they were shure of being a towne granted in the first place. Secondly, I being the first that had a house in Salem, (and neither had any hand in nameing either that or any other towne,) and myself, with those that were with me, being all from the western part of England, desire this western name of Budleigh, a market town in Devonshire, and neere unto the sea, as wee are heere in this place, and where my-self was borne. . . ."

The petition was signed by thirty-three or thirty-four persons besides Conant, but was apparently not granted, as Beverly is still Beverly, and has been all the time.

The English town of Beverley in the East Riding of Yorkshire, from whence the name of the Massachusetts town probably came, though the two names are not spelled identically, was once noted for its beavers, and the name is said to be a development of Beverlac, meaning lake of beavers, though I have also read that it indicates a beaver meadow or beaver lee. But Beverly, Massachusetts, seems to have been noted in the past not for beavers but for beans.

From the many mistakes which were made in naming towns, it might be concluded that the early legislators were indifferent to the matter, but the records show that they took the business seriously. They demurred when asked to legalize the name of New London, Connecticut, suggesting that the town be called Fair Harbor instead; but to this the inhabitants would not consent, preferring to adhere to the Indian name Pequot, or to one of the other aboriginal names which they had tried, if they could not have the one of their choice. Evidently it was thought that the New Londoners wanted to adopt the name of the great English metropolis as bait, or had delusions of expected grandeur; but at length they succeeded in convincing the authorities that their desire for the name was based on affection, not vainglory, and on March 24, 1658, the place was named New London. The act by which this was done constitutes so unusual a baptismal certificate that I quote it in full:

"Whereas it hath been a commendable practice of the inhabitants of all the colonies of these parts, that as this country hath its denomination from our dear native country of England, and hence is called New England; so the planters, in their first settling of new plantations, have given names to those plantations of some cities and towns of England, thereby intending to keep up and leave to posterity the memorial of several places of note there, as *Boston, Hartford, Windsor, York, Ipswich, Braintree, Exeter*. This court considering, that there hath yet no place in any of the colonies, been named in memory of the city of London, there being a new plantation within this jurisdiction of Connecticut, settled upon the fair river Monhegin, in the Pequot country, it being an excellent harbour and a fit and convenient place for future trade, it being also the only place which the English of these parts have possessed by conquest, and that by a very just war, upon the great and warlike people, the Pequots, and therefore, they might thereby leave to posterity the memory of that renowned city of London, from whence we had our transportation, have thought fit, in honour to that famous city, to call the said plantation New London."

The Connecticut men who conquered the Pequot country, as mentioned in this resolution, were rewarded by the colony with grants of land, a custom which was followed after the Narragansett War, when much of the territory now comprising the town of Voluntown was granted to the officers and men who served in that war. The grant was made in 1696, and the town incorporated in 1720. Voluntown is, of course, a withered form of Volunteers' Town.

In the seventeenth century the act of the colonial court or assembly in authorizing the name was often the only governmental action taken in the matter of town organization.

Other New England towns beside New London have used different names, some adopting new ones as often as burglars and cutpurses are supposed to change theirs. The classically named town of Troy, Maine, has had no fewer than five names. When the settlement was organized into a plantation, it was called Bridgestown after its first proprietor. It was incorporated in 1812 under the name of Kingsville, in honor of the man who later became the first governor of Maine. During the next fifteen years it bore the brief, bright name of Joy, followed by that of Montgomery. The final change to Troy was made in 1827.

John Shepherd, a native of Foxborough, Massachusetts, who died in 1809 at the age of one hundred and nine, dwelt for over a century in the place where he was born, and during that time lived in two counties and four different towns without moving once.

The first name of a town was often admittedly provisional, and in some instances was merely a number, as Township Number Four. Occasionally a place had several names before it was even settled. Gloucester, our oldest fishing port, was called Wingaersheek by the Indians. Champlain, who discovered the harbor in 1606, gave it the name of Le Beauport. Then came Captain John Smith, who explored the locality in 1614 and left a record of his visit by calling it Tragabigzanda, after a Turkish lady who saved him from slavery. This was the name it was known by until Prince Charles rechristened it Cape Ann, in honor of his mother, Princess Ann of Denmark. Smith dedicated his map of New England (1616) to Prince Charles, afterward Charles I, with the request that he change the

Indian names. "So favorable was your most renowned brother, Prince Henry, to all generous designs, that in my discovery of Virginia, I presumed to call two nameless headlands after my sovereign's heirs, Cape Henry and Cape Charles. Since then, it being my chance to range some parts of America, whereof I here present your highness the description in a map, my humble suit is, you would please to change their barbarous names for such English, as posterity may say, Prince Charles was their godfather."

The first colonists came in 1623, but it was not until 1642 that the settlement was incorporated, and Cape Ann was embraced within its limits. Gloucester was chosen for its name because many of the settlers were natives of the old English cathedral town of Gloucester.

An outstanding example of the confusion of names which may result from numerous changes is presented by the Maine towns of Biddeford and Saco, which lie across from each other on opposite banks of the Saco River. Both sides of the river were once called Saco, but in 1718 the name was changed to Biddeford, after Bideford in Devon, England. In 1762 the east side was incorporated separately as the town of Pepperellborough, in compliment to Sir William Pepperell, who was at one time a large landowner in the town. Then in

1805 Pepperellborough was dropped in favor of the old name of Saco.

Repetition of place names, which is of frequent occurrence in New England, is sometimes confusing. Once in his youth my father and one of his brothers became lost while driving home from a dance at Curtis's Grove in Medfield, Massachusetts, to Framingham. Their horse did not know the way any better than they did. After spending the dull watches of the night wandering around back-country roads, they at length came to a house. In answer to their summons, a man put his head out of an upper window and asked what they wanted at such an hour.

"What town is this?" inquired my father.

"Dover," was the answer.

"Dover, Maine, or Dover, New Hampshire?" asked the brother.

"Dover, Massachusetts, you damn fool!" came the disgusted reply.

The following is from a match book cover picked up recently in the Village Green Café in Plymouth, New Hampshire: "Now let us get this straight. You are in Plymouth, New Hampshire. Plymouth is in the geographical center of New Hampshire. Its altitude is 483 feet. The Pilgrims *did not* land here. Plymouth Rock is not situated in town. It had to be near the Seacoast. The Mayflower *did not* anchor in our harbor because we haven't any harbor. We have as good, if not better, neighbors than any other town. Our visitors are of the kind who make us proud to have them around. Our weather is regular New England weather. Ninety per cent of all the weather in the world passes through our Main Street every February. It is then distributed to the weaker communities in diluted doses."

Duplication of names was not always the result of transplantation. Like the dedications of books, the naming of towns was often done to honor an individual, perhaps in the hope of securing a patron who might benefit the place in some way, either by an outright gift to the town, or by the exercise of political influence favorable to it; though more often than not it was done out of pure admiration or gratitude. Popular heroes were frequently complimented in this way. Every New England state has its Washington, and other well-liked Revolutionary figures such as Franklin, Adams, Hancock, Warren, and Jefferson, were repeatedly put on the map. Among the English statesmen and warriors who were honored before the Revolution were Marlborough, Pitt, Wolfe, and Walpole.

On the other hand, Worcester, Massachusetts, was given that name as a direct political insult to Sir Edmund Andross, the colonial governor. It was named in memory of the Worcester where Cromwell whipped the Pretender, afterward Charles II, making him run for his life and wrecking for awhile the hopes of the Stuarts.

At the time of the incorporation of the town of Franklin, Massachusetts, in 1788, a friend of Benjamin Franklin wrote to him in Paris that, a town in the vicinity of Boston having chosen his name by which to be known to the world, the writer presumed "as they had no bell with which to summon the people to meeting on the Sabbath, a present of such an instrument from him would be very acceptable, especially as they were about erecting a new meeting house." Franklin replied that he presumed the people in Franklin were more fond of sense than of sound, and accordingly sent them a handsome donation of books.

The Rev. Benjamin Woodbridge, for whom Woodbridge, Connecticut, was named, gave the town a copy of Whitby's *Commentary of the New Testament* in token of his appreciation of the honor.

When in 1761 Lord Coleraine of Ireland heard that a town in Massachusetts had been named after him he was so pleased that he sent the inhabitants a splendid bell. The bell, however, never reached them, for the agent to whom it was entrusted proved unfaithful. Barber, writing in 1839, said the bell was believed to be in existence still and in use by a Boston church. Today Colerain enjoys the distinction of having more covered bridges than any place in New England. There are in the township six of the old wooden structures.

The town of Berkeley, Massachusetts, refused the gift of an organ from Bishop Berkeley, because "an organ is an instrument of the Devil for entrapping men's souls." So the bishop gave the organ to Trinity Church in Newport, where it can be seen today surmounted by the crown of England, with a bishop's miter on each side. The organ has been enlarged and renovated, of course, since it was presented to the church in 1733, but the central part is the original instrument.

Prenatal gifts have in a few cases influenced the choice of place names. The town of Holden, Massachusetts, incorporated in 1740, commemorates the Hon. Samuel Holden, a director of the Bank of England, who was a liberal benefactor of the literary and religious institutions of New England. He transmitted to New England for charitable purposes books and bills of exchange to the amount of £4,847. After his decease, his widow and daughter sent over for the same noble and pious uses the sum of £5,585. With a part of this latter sum Holden Chapel at Harvard College was erected in 1745. These gifts were not made, of course, in expectation that the family name would be given to a town.

In another case the present of a sword resulted in the naming of a town for the donor. This was Charlestown, New Hampshire, one of the oldest villages in the western part of that state, which was originally known as Number Four. In 1747 the small garrison stationed there, consisting of thirty men commanded by Captain Phineas Stevens, was attacked by four hundred French and Indians. In demanding the surrender of the outpost, the French commander pointed to the overwhelming odds in his favor and to the almost certain massacre of the defenders that would follow the fall of the fort. Captain Stevens replied, "I can assure you, my men are not afraid to die." The fight raged for three days, at the end of which time the attempt to take the place was abandoned, and the French returned to Canada. Sir Charles Knowles, a British naval officer at Boston, hearing of the bravery of Captain Stevens, presented him with an elegant sword, and when the town came to be incorporated it was named Charlestown in honor of Sir Charles.

Before and after the Revolution there were many migrations from one place to another in New England, and persons moving in a group to fresh woods often took with them the name of the town of their origin. Sometimes they added the prefix "New" to the old name, but frequently they did not even bother to do this and took the old title straight without adornment. This stereotyping of names may perhaps argue a lack of originality, but in most cases it was probably done from nostalgia or a desire on the part of the junior colony to honor the senior settlement from which it sprang. It was the same motive which prompted the early colonists to adopt the names of their native towns in the old country. Then, too, distances were relatively much greater in New England in those far-off times, and places with the same name were more widely severed than they are today.

Many Vermont names are duplications of Connecticut names. Some of these are contained in the following list, which is by no means complete. In some instances the towns were organized and held their first meetings in Connecticut before any move was made to Vermont. In addition to these mass exoduses, Vermont was also a great stamping ground for individuals whose habits had become unsettled by army life during the Revolution. Renegade husbands from Connecticut and other parts of New England fled to Vermont, or to the regions beyond the "formidable Hudson." With them sometimes went recreant girls, possessing such names as Desire, Submit, Thankful, Deliverance, and Content. But here is a list of duplicate place names, the majority of them taken directly from Connecticut.

Bethel	Fair Haven	Pomfret
Bolton	Franklin	Sharon
Bristol	Glastonbury	Salisbury
Brookfield	Granby	Stamford
Burlington	Guilford	Vernon
Canaan	Hartford	Wallingford
Colchester	Hartland	Warren
Cornwall	Huntington	Waterbury
Coventry	Middletown	Weston
Derby	New Haven	Windham
East Haven	Norwich	Windsor
Fairfield	Plainfield	Woodstock

When the founders of a new settlement came from several towns, they sometimes made up a new name that was a composite of the names of the places from which they had migrated. Harwinton, Connecticut, is an example of this. It was settled by people from Hartford, Windsor, and Farmington.

Since the early days New England place names have multiplied and spread all over the country, and some thirty islands in the Pacific Ocean bear the names of Nantucket sea captains and ship owners. Altogether, more than four hundred Pacific reefs and islands owe their names to American whalemen.

When a new town was created from part of an old one, it was common practice for the new place to take the parental name with the addition of a directional prefix, such as North, East, South, or West. Dozens of examples of this are to be found throughout New England. The practice came into use, of course, on the breaking up of the ancient towns. When the outlying parishes or villages of a town reached a point of development where it was felt that they could deal with their own problems better if set off by themselves, they were cut adrift and made into separate political entities. Because of geographical proximity to the parent town, the offspring town could not take the old name by itself, so the directional device was frequently used. Sometimes the newly created town took only a part of the original name, usually the termination, which, combined with one of the prefixes mentioned, made such neighborhood names as Northborough (from Marlborough), Easton (once part of Taunton), Southbridge (from Sturbridge), and Westford (from Chelmsford), all in Massachusetts. While this combining form is not so clearly indicative of relationship as the other, it saved a town from having a double-barreled name and sometimes gave it a shorter one than the original. Not a few of the names created in this way are as condensed as cable addresses.

Occasionally one finds a town with a name obviously derived from the town's situation and bearing in relation to some other place, and yet that other place is difficult to discover. One looks in vain around the town of East Hampton, Connecticut, which in horse and buggy days was the center of the sleigh-bell industry, for a place from which the name could have been derived. There is plainly no connection between it and the town of Hampton in the same state, because the two places are thirty or forty air miles apart, and East Hampton does not lie to the east of Hampton but to the west of it. A reading of the history of the town solved the mystery of this orphan name for me. The place was settled by people from Eastham on Cape Cod, who brought the name with them. These people left the Cape to settle on the Connecticut River because they did not want their sons to go to sea; but their sons, of course, went to sea just the same. East Hampton really ought to be spelled with a small *h* and as one word, but long usage has established the capital letter and the two-word form.

Apart from the four cardinal points of the compass, few other directions on the card have been used in the fabrication of place names, and these have been employed so sparingly that about the only examples which readily come to mind are Northeast Harbor and Southwest Harbor on Mount Desert Island. They were so named on account of their locations at the northeast and southwest sides respectively of the entrance to Somes Sound at the southerly end of the island.

The Indians also used names which described the position of places, or their direction from points already known. From their own tribal territory, a place might be "beyond the mountain" (Housatonic), "land beyond the river" (Agamenticus), "the east land" (Abnaki, Wampanoag), "the halfway place" (Nashaway). And, as in the case of the whites, they did not hesitate to give the same name to more than one place.

Amid all the copying that has been done of place names and of their prefixes and suffixes, one occasionally finds a town which claims the distinction of having a name that is unique. The people of Henniker, New Hampshire, which was named for a London merchant, assert that their town is the only Henniker in the world; and the inhabitants of Winterport, Maine, on the Penobscot River, will tell you that a letter addressed simply to Winterport, U. S. A., will reach that town, as there is no other Winterport anywhere. One hopes that these towns and others like them will never suffer any infringement of title.

Many tiny villages and districts in New England are so obscure that their names are neither widely known nor do they often get into print, save on signboards, or on very large-scale maps, or in the pages of country weekly newspapers. Yet many of these names are among the most picturesque and curious in New England. One finds them everywhere, but for illustrative purposes let us see what a single state has to offer.

We find that Connecticut has a Purgatory, a Satan's Kingdom, and a Devil's Hopyard. Here also is found Poverty, Hardscrabble, and Vexation, all, no doubt, realistically named. As an offset to these, mention may be made of the less barren and unfruitful names of Enterprise, Success, Dividend, and Equivalent. There is a Sodom, but no Gomorrah, and a Nineveh, Nod, and Zoar. What kind of places, one wonders, are Bashbish, Ballahack, Bungay, and Bedlam? Other interesting names are Puckshire, Puffingham, and Podunk; Samp Mortar, Shuttle Meadow, and Stadley Rough. Then there are the pleasantly riparian titles such as Rope Ferry, Bend of River, Pistol Point Bar, and Weir Town. Gypseyville suggests a wild and moory camp site; Donkeyville a place of thistles, and Gallows

Hill a grim spot where men were publicly strangled; while the mind is switched to pleasanter associations with the mention of Fluteville, Music Vale, and Bell Town. There is atmosphere in the names Above All, Break Neck, Johnny Cake, and Quail Trap; Isinglass, Old Furnace Hollow, and Kettletown. One hardly expects to come across street names in the country, but there is a rural district in Connecticut which is not inappropriately named Lovely Street, and in the town of Scotland there is a district which, not too unhappily, perhaps, is called Pinch Street. It is safe to say that interesting bits of history or legend probably cling to most of these names.

The following story is told of the place with the sulphurous name of Satan's Kingdom, which is a rough and hilly district in the eastern part of the town of New Hartford, where in the early days the few inhabitants were said in a measure to have been shut out from the rest of mankind. "An inhabitant of the town invited one of his neighbors who lived within the limits of this district, to go and hear Mr. Marsh, the first minister who was settled in the town. He was prevailed upon to go to church in the forenoon. In the course of his prayer, Mr. Marsh, among other things, prayed that *Satan's kingdom might be destroyed*. It appears that the inhabitant of this district, took the expression in a literal and tangible sense, probably never having heard the expression used but in reference to the district wherein he resided. Being asked to go to meeting in the afternoon, he refused, stating that Mr. Marsh had insulted him. 'For blast him,' he cried, 'when he prayed for the destruction of Satan's Kingdom, he very well knew all my interests lay there.' "

The map of New England has been very hospitable to the Devil.

Some names have sunk so low in the social scale that steps have been taken to eradicate them. The honest Anglo-Saxon word hog, which was very popular with our ancestors, is one that has fallen into bad odor. It was used to name islands, streams, and hills. One of the most prominent and beautiful islands in Casco Bay was formerly Hog Island. The muddy river which flows through the grounds of the state capital at Hartford has for years been informally known as Hog River. And many an arched New England hill has borne the name Hogback. In one case it was proposed that Hogback should be changed to Mount Bacon.

The origin of many place names is shrouded in mystery. This is the case with the attractively named Massachusetts island of Martha's Vineyard. In the seventeenth century it was known indifferently as Martin's Vineyard or Martha's Vineyard, but nobody knows who Martin and Martha were, or what they had to do, if anything, with the island, beyond the grape-growing suggestion contained in the name. It is possible that one name was derived from the other, but which came first cannot now be told. In any case, one is glad that Martha got the upper hand of Martin, and one hopes that she was a real person and not a mythical one, as few women have had their names singled out for geographical honors. Bartholomew Gosnold, the navigator, who is supposed to have christened the vineyard for Martha, seems to have been an exceptionally gallant man, for he also gave a feminine name to the neighboring string of islands, which he called the Elizabeth Islands in honor of Queen Elizabeth. From these islands Gosnold shipped the first cargo ever to be exported from New England. He sent home a shipload of cedar and sassafras.

Duke's County, which is made up of Martha's Vineyard, the Elizabeth Islands, and their satellites, is one of Massachusetts' two insular counties, the other being Nantucket. This county name has an interesting history. None of these islands came under the jurisdiction of any of the New England colonial governments, but belonged to New York, and as such were included in a grant of New York which Charles II made to his brother the Duke of York. In 1683 the Provincial Assembly of New York divided the province into counties, among them King's County, Queen's County, and Duke's County. These county names have survived to this day. King's is now Brooklyn, Queen's lies next to it on Long Island, and Duke's is Martha's Vineyard. By the charter of William and Mary, which reached Boston in 1692, the islands of Duke's County were detached from New York and given to Massachusetts. In 1695, Nantucket, which had been part of Duke's County, was made a separate county by itself.

Not many leagues from Martha's Vineyard and the Elizabeth Islands is another place with a feminine name—Point Judith, at the entrance to Narragansett Bay. There is no mystery as to how it came by its name. It was named for Judith Quincy, the wife of John Hull of Boston, one of the few early New England silversmiths about whom anything is known. In 1652 he was made mint master of Massachusetts and made a fortune coining the famous pine-tree shillings and sixpences.

The explanations of the origins of some place names are so unsatisfactory as to leave one feeling quite as much in the dark as ever about them. The town of Duxbury, Massachusetts, is thought to have been named for Captain Miles Standish, and in an old work it is said, "The probable etymology of the present name is Dux and borough, as it is stated that it was named in honor of Capt. Standish, the *dux* or military leader of the colony, and one of the first settlers of the place." This explanation is difficult to swallow, and the historian of Duxbury repudiates it in favor of the theory that it was probably named for Duxbury Hall, the seat of the Standish family in England. It may be so, but one remembers that Roxbury was so called because of the rocks there, and one wonders if Duxbury may not have been named for the ducks which abounded in the waters adjacent to the town. But this, of course, is just a guess, too.

Since the origin of many place names is not a matter of written record but merely of oral tradition, the history of some names now known will probably be lost. Anyone who has been attracted strongly enough by a name to make inquiries concerning its origin knows how difficult it often is to find anyone who can tell him anything about it. At the easterly end of the Maine coast is an anchorage called Bailey's Mistake, a name which aroused my curiosity. Who was Bailey, I wondered, and what was his mistake? It was only by the most persistent efforts that I was able to get an answer. Years ago, it seems, a certain Captain Bailey was trying to find the St. Croix River and sailed into the anchorage that now bears his name, thinking it was the entrance to the river, which he had missed by six miles. Another version is that he was seeking refuge in Cutler Harbor. But in either case he was mistaken and suffered shipwreck in the anchorage.

Of the various influences which have operated to make the place names of New England, it is not surprising to find that the Bible has exerted a strong sway. It was a favorite source of personal names, as any visitor to old New England burial grounds can testify. Except for the surnames on the stones, one might almost be reading an ancient directory of Joppa or Jericho. For here one finds such familiar and unfamiliar scriptural names as Ezra, Neriah, Zillah, Ashael, Azariah, Joab, Heber, Asa, Shadrack, Abinadab, Jepthah, Philemon, Jachin, Hepzibah, and many others, some of which the visitor may never have known existed in the Bible. Surely a great many of them must have been chosen by the haphazard method of opening the Bible at random and taking the first name that met the eye.

No less does the map suggest that New England and the Holy Land were once in a tangle. Among New England names of Levantine origin are Lebanon, Hebron, Hermon, Carmel, Salem, Goshen, Gilead, Jericho, Jerusalem, Sharon, Bozrah, Bethel,

Bethlehem, Rehoboth, and Canaan. It is recollected that the Rev. Israel Woodward of Wolcott, Connecticut, once preached a thanksgiving sermon in which he compared the state of Connecticut to the land of Canaan. In one respect, he mentioned there was a striking similarity; the land of Canaan was rocky, and this was very much the case with Connecticut, at least that part of it in which Wolcott was situated. Bronson Alcott, it will be recalled was born in this rocky, upland town.

The Massachusetts town with the unusual name of Rehoboth was named by the Rev. Samuel Newman, who, as mentioned in another chapter, had a premonition of his death. He moved from Weymouth, Massachusetts, with part of his parish in 1644. The following year the new settlement was incorporated by the scriptural name of Rehoboth, which was selected by Mr. Newman, because, he said, "the Lord has made room for us."

Bangor, Maine, was named for the hymn tune, "Bangor."

Even stronger than the clerical influence on New England names has been the influence of the sea. Naturally this is most marked along our shores, where are shoals of amphibious names compounded of such maritime words as harbor, haven, port, cove, bay, sound, cape, point, head, neck, beach, shore, pier, and landing. A great tide of salty titles breaks along the coast of hundred-harbored Maine, where there are more islands than tales in *The Arabian Nights.* Nowhere but on the coast or near it would you be likely to find villages named Starboard, Head Tide, Seal Harbor, and Mast Landing, or insular names like Nautilus Island, Shipstern Island, Whaleboat Island, Wreck Island, and Ballast Island.

Less salty but none the less interesting are the names of other Maine islands: Tumble Down Dick, the Cuckolds, the Virgin's Breasts, Hurricane Island, Burnt Island, Devil's Island, the Hypocrites, Ironbound Island, Negro Island, Junk of Pork, Isle au Haut, the Cranberry Islands, St. Helena, Littlejohn, Big Pot, Bombazine Island, Jones' Garden, Pope's Folly, Jordan's Delight, Ten Pound Island, No Man's Land, Powderhorn Island, Two Bush Island, Rogue's Island, and Brimstone Island. When it comes to throwing place names around, Maine can hold its own with any state.

The influence of the sea has also penetrated inland. Almost without looking, one could tell that towns named after the Chinese city of Canton were named in the period when Yankee ships and Yankee sailors were extending our maritime commerce to the Orient.

It is possible that a few towns may have been christened as ships are christened—with a bottle.

But what their names are I do not know. The bottle ritual was used in naming a stream, Lull's Brook, in Hartland, Vermont. Timothy Lull of Dummerston, the first settler of Hartland, came up the Connecticut River in a canoe in 1763, with his wife and children, and landed at the mouth of the brook. Taking out a bottle and breaking it in the presence of his family, he gave his own peaceful name to the stream.

Many places have derived their names from trees which may once have been among their prominent geographical features. Thus we have Ashfield, Elmhurst, Beechwood, Pineville, Sprucehead, Cedar Grove, Juniper Point, Oakland, Appleton, Locustville, Buttonwoods, Chestnut Hill, Willows, Maplegrove, Birches, Hawthorne, Magnolia, Mount Holly, Walnut Hill, Plumtrees, Lindenwood, Gilead, and others. In explanation of the last name, it should be stated that the town of Gilead, Maine, is said to have taken its name not from the Bible but from a great balm of Gilead tree which stood in the middle of the town.

In this list it would be proper, I think, to include the town which was named after a famous botanist. The town is Linneus, Maine, which was granted by Massachusetts while Maine was still part of the Bay State to endow a professorship of botany, and was named after the celebrated eighteenth-century

Swedish botanist, Linnaeus, whose name came from the linden tree.

Some place names have come from the local industry which has been largely responsible for the making of the place. Ivoryton, Connecticut, where most of the ivory keys for the piano trade were made, is an example of this. The ivory business was started there many years ago with the making of ivory combs and toothpicks. But more often it has been the industrialist rather than the industry which has been memorialized. Hazardville, Connecticut, was not so named because there were powder mills there but because the manufacturer engaged in that perilous business was Colonel Hazard.

The fortuitous way in which a place sometimes acquired a name is illustrated by the case of Waterloo, New Hampshire, which was named for Waterloo, New York. Two New Hampshire deputy sheriffs chased a fugitive from New Hampshire into New York and captured him at Waterloo. So impressed were the deputies with the beauty of the village of Waterloo lying at the foot of Seneca Lake that they not only brought back their man but also the name of the place where they caught him.

Indian place names were almost without exception descriptive. Many were melodious and pleasing, and it is a pity to have lost them. Others, which were not only unattractive but also difficult to spell and to pronounce and had only their aboriginality to recommend them, were wisely dropped. James Russell Lowell said he was no fanatic for Indian nomenclature, for the name of his native district had been Pigsgusset. While some people think that every Indian name should have been retained at all costs, it would seem that on the whole the fittest have survived, in company with a few that should have been allowed to die.

Probably the most extraordinary and curious example of Indian name-making that has come down to us is the name of a small lake in Webster, Massachusetts—Lake Charcoggagoggchaugagoggchaubunagungamaugg. This impossible name has all the earmarks of conjurer's gibberish or of having been invented as a joke, but it is a perfectly legitimate Indian name, which was accepted as given above by the great Indian scholar, Professor Horsford of Harvard. He said it meant boundary fishing place. "Believe-It-Or-Not" Ripley once used the name as spelled here, but I have also seen it written in the abbreviated form Charcogg—etc.—maugg. Small boys who used to go swimming in the lake, which lies partly in Connecticut, called it Junkermug, though now, I believe, it is usually referred to as Webster Lake. If you can pronounce the full Indian name, you are to be congratulated. The only person from whose tongue I ever heard it roll trippingly was a man who lived in Dudley, the town next to Webster. He was a minister who had kept in training on Bible names like Nebuchadnezzar.

Many of the Indian names which have survived have suffered so terribly from mutilation as to be hardly recognizable for what they were originally, and in some cases have completely lost their reason for being attached to particular places. Except for a little crude picture-writing, the Indians had no written language, and the spelling of the names was left to the settlers, who, as we have seen, were not good spellers. There was no teamwork among them. It was a case of every man for himself. And so we find the same name spelled many different ways, with varying numbers of syllables.

How the civilizing process sometimes works on a barbaric name is seen in the case of Ragged Island on the Maine coast. Not the Ragged Island owned by Edna St. Vincent Millay in Casco Bay, but the island off the entrance to Penobscot Bay on which is the small fishing village of Criehaven. To judge by the name alone, a person might reasonably suppose it was descriptive and that the place was called Ragged Island because it had a tattered and torn coast line or because it was so thinly clad with soil that the bare rocks showed like the flesh of a beggar seen through his rags. But the island originally bore the Indian name Racketash, which the whites metamorphosed according to its sound into Ragged Ass, or Ragged Arse, as I have seen it spelled, until at length it became simply Ragged Island.

Amusing legends are linked to some of the Indian names. Hockamock Head, the gray and craggy headland on the inside passage between Boothbay Harbor and Bath, Maine, received its name from a baroque incident which occurred there in colonial times. Near it was a small settlement which was attacked and burned by the Indians. On the appearance of the savages, the settlers abandoned their homes and fled along the promontory, where the cliffs and steeps made a series of natural defenses. As they raced across the neck toward their stronghold, the Indians pursued them hotly.

"A Scotchman," says a Maine historian, "less fleet of foot than his fellows from age or corpulence, his head protected by a wig of antique size and fashion, brought up the lagging rear, and soon fell within grasp of the pursuing red man, whose outstretched hand laid hold of the flowing wig for a head of hair which promised a magnificent trophy to the scalping knife. But to the surprise and consternation of the savage, the periwig clave to his hold, while the apparently headless body still ran on, leaping from steep to steep, utterly indifferent to what he had left behind. The astonished savage, believing he had been running a race with a devil, suddenly stopped, and dropping the wig in superstitious horror, turned to fly in the opposite direction, crying to his comrades, 'Hockamock! Hockamock! The devil! The devil!' "

On the easterly side of the Schoodic Peninsula, also on the Maine coast, is a stream emptying into the sea which is known officially on the map as Wonsqueak, but is called by the natives One Screech. According to one local tradition, an Indian who found his squaw was unfaithful took her out in his canoe and heaved her overboard. Before sinking beneath the ripples forever, she gave only one screech.

Lydia Huntley Sigourney, the Hartford poetess, wrote a poem on Indian names, in which she calls attention to the number which have survived, particularly in the case of our rivers and other bodies of water.

> Ye say, they have passed away,
> That noble race and brave;
> That their light canoes have vanished,
> From off the crested wave;

That, 'mid the forest where they roamed,
There rings no hunter's shout;
But their name is on your waters,—
Ye may not wash it out.

Henry James thought that the names of our rivers were better than those of our towns. But one thing he could not put up with was the custom of sometimes naming rivers for towns, the taking by the greater of the comparatively common little names of the less. For this reason he objected to the name of the Farmington River in Connecticut. The town of Farmington he thought delightful, but villages, fords, and bridges, he declared, are not the godparents of the element which made them possible, they are much rather the godchildren. On this point one is inclined to agree with him.

TO HARK BACK TO THE PAST

IT is a favorite custom with old New Englanders to hark back to the olden times, but there is nothing surprising in this, for New England has a rich and varied history. Delve in the ashes of her past almost anywhere and you are bound to unurn odd and interesting items. Take the illustrated weekly papers for the year 1860, for example. They give a graphic picture of American life in general and

New England life in particular that is worth a backward glance.

In that year the country was in the throes of the presidential campaign which culminated in the election of Abraham Lincoln. The Prince of Wales, afterward Edward VII, a youth of eighteen, visited the United States and was royally entertained, especially at Boston. The wonderful new ocean liner, "Great Eastern," figured repeatedly in the news, as did other sidewheelers which were busy pouring immigrants, mostly from Ireland, into the country. Literary critics spoke sharply to Mr. Longfellow about writing on European rather than American themes; while a Boston publisher issued a new and enlarged edition of Walt Whitman's *Leaves of Grass*, and the young *Atlantic Monthly* won the highest praise.

News from the Pacific coast came by way of the pony express. Indian fighting and buffalo hunting were favorite subjects of picturization. It was the year of the Heenan-Sayers fight, of several notable horse races, and aquatic sports of all kinds. A man gained fame by rowing from Boston to New York in a wherry. Many veterans of the War of 1812 were still alive, and at least one New Englander who fought at Bunker Hill. The career of William Walker, the filibusterer, was terminated by his execution in Honduras. There were numerous shipwrecks, disastrous fires, and boiler explosions. Crime, including political graft, was a serious problem.

All these and many other matters were covered by the illustrated weeklies, which also printed lurid serials, gloated over scandals, and shamelessly puffed patent remedies, which seem always to have been a moving force in our history. Many features popular with the journals of 1860 are characteristic of our papers today; though editors now have not the mania they had then for using pictures of insane asylums. It made no difference where the asylum was located, whether at home or abroad, an editor was happy if he could run a drawing with the caption, "Beautiful View of the Mad House at *X*."

From the pages of two national weeklies of large circulation—*Frank Leslie's Weekly* and the *New York Illustrated News*, both for 1860—come the following items of news touching New England. Amusingly old-fashioned in style, they give a partial but clear picture of certain phases of New England life in the year before the outbreak of the Civil War.

"On Saturday last, Miss Esty of West Newton, near Boston, went into a neighboring shrubbery to pick some strawberries. Not returning, a search was made, but although the entire population went out in the search, nothing has been seen or heard of her. She is of dark complexion, has dark hair and eyes, and a slight squint."

"The Treasurer of Amherst College, has lately received from Mr. David Sears, of Boston, a heretofore liberal benefactor of the college, a small and carefully sealed box, with the instruction that it is not to be opened for one hundred years, on the pain of a forfeiture of the gift which it contains. Speculation is at fault as to the contents and the reason for the accompanying condition. The shrewdest guess is that the box contains deeds of real estate in Boston now under lease for one hundred years, but then to be transferred to the college. But let us be patient till 1960, and then we shall know, says the Springfield *Republican*."

"Hawthorne and Whittier are to lead off in the October number of the *Atlantic Monthly*, we hear, and the brilliant writer of *The Amber Gods* and *Sir Rohan's Ghost*, Miss Prescott, begins a new story of some length in the November number. Mrs. Stowe's new romance is also to appear shortly in the *Atlantic*. Constant in the galaxy, emitting light in the pages of the monthly are Longfellow, Emerson, Whittier, Holmes, Hawthorne, Lowell,

Rose Terry, Mrs. Stowe, Miss Prescott, and Fanny Kemble."

"A soiree at Saratoga is an every day occurrence, and is soon forgotten; but a grand ball of the season like that of last Tuesday night, creates a sensation in all circles. . . . The ball room of Union Hall is without doubt the largest of any hotel of the country, being over two hundred feet long and seventy-five feet wide. . . . There were two bands present—Hall's Boston Brass Band and the Lowell Brass Band—one on either side of the room. Mr. D. C. Hall played upon a bugle of gold, which was presented him some time since by the Lowell Band."

"The Democratic State Central Committee has resolved to celebrate the visit of Senator Stephen A. Douglas to Rhode Island by holding a monster meeting and clam bake on Thursday, at Rocky Point, a favorite resort for excursion parties. The Point is fifteen miles distant from Providence, being the most beautiful location on Narragansett Bay. The announcement in the public journals stated that Mr. Douglas would review one of the oldest and most democratic of Rhode Island institutions—a clam bake.

"The most extensive arrangements that could be effected were made to accommodate the thousands that were expected to visit Rocky Point on this the most auspicious event in the political history of Rhode Island.

"All the steamers plying between Providence, Newport, and adjacent places, were called into requisition, to accommodate the multitude that were anxious to take part in the ovation; but notwithstanding the number of excursion boats provided by the Committee, thousands were unable to get to the Point. From an early hour in the morning till late in the afternoon the boats landed not less than 30,000 people, while at least 20,000 more reached the grove by the land route, in all sorts of conveyances. Enterprising Yankee peddlers did a brisk business in disposing of photographs and medals of the 'Little Giant' and an eccentric individual, known by the cognomen of the 'General,' was actively employed in selling a song, composed in twelve minutes, on the monster clam bake and the arrival of Douglas."

"A meeting was held at Newport on Saturday evening to give expression to the sympathy entertained for the patriot Garibaldi, and the cause for which he is at present struggling in Italy, and to take the initiatory steps toward raising a subscription to afford him material aid. The attendance was quite numerous."

"Our correspondent, writing from Newport, says:

NEWPORT, R. I., August 6th, 1860.

"The tide of fashionables that usually throng places of summer resort, has been, during the past week, setting in very strongly toward Newport, and the hotel-proprietors who had begun to frown darkly at the prospect before them are now all smiles, as the chances for a full harvest thus materially brighten. For this change they are indebted, in a measure, to Senator Douglas, whose arrival at the Atlantic House, on Thursday last, brought a crowd of party men, lion hunters, members of the Press, pleasure-seekers, and hangers-on.

"In addition, we have a grand council of the savants of science in convention assembled, under the title of 'Fourteenth Annual Session of the American Association for the Advancement of Science,' which has added considerably to the number of visitors.

"The Press is here in strong force. We noticed representatives from the *Tribune*, *Herald*, *Times*, and *World* of New York; *Post*, *Courier*, and *Herald*, of Boston; *Post*, *Press*, and *Courant*, of Hartford; *Palladium*, of New Haven; *Press* and *Post*, of Providence, and others.

"Harriet Hosmer, the sculptress, is at the Bellevue House. Miss Mitchell, the Nantucket astronomer, is with her."

"Among the papers read in the Scientific Congress at Newport, on Saturday, was one by Prof. Agassiz, on Methods of Zoology; one by Prof. Bache, on the Magnetism of the Moon; one by C. B. Hitchcock, Esq., on the Geology of Newport, and one by Capt. Hunt, on War in its Scientific Aspect. No division into sections took place, and only one session was held—the savants in the afternoon making a visit to the fort. Great interest was felt in the paper of Prof. Agassiz, as it was thought he might touch upon the theory of Darwin in his Origin of Species; but the great crowd which flocked to hear it was disappointed, as he scarcely approached it."

"The Lowell *Citizen* tells a romantic story about a young lady of that city, who was for many years an assistant teacher in one of the grammar schools there. She has left her home in company with her sister, on a journey of over a thousand miles, to meet and marry a man she has never seen. The engagement was brought about by means of a piece of poetry written by her while residing in a neighboring city, and published in the local paper of that place. The article, signed by a fictitious name, was seen by the gentleman and so much admired that he wrote to the address, and the correspondence, thus begun, was kept up for nearly two years, and has resulted as above. We hope the young lady has not made a fool of herself. Such matches as this do not usually end well—and the odds are terribly against her. She is a brave girl however—woman rather, if we may judge by the 'many years' she has been a teacher—and deserves to get a good husband, after traveling so far to find one."

"Mr. Dean Symonds, of Vermont, came here a few days since to look at New York. Having heard of rascally hotel keepers, he would not trust his money with the landlord, but carried it in his pantaloon pockets. On Thursday he went to see the *American Cousin* at Laura Keene's, and was highly delighted at the piece. What was his dismay, when he went into a saloon to take a drink, to find that some needy 'American Cousin' had borrowed nearly $500 of him without having the decency of leaving his address."

"The family of Michael Quinnan, in Suffield, Connecticut, was poisoned on Tuesday by eating freely of toadstools, having mistaken them for mushrooms. Two of the children are already dead, and Mrs. Quinnan and the youngest child, two years of age, are not expected to survive."

"Mrs. Wright, of Massachusetts, was lately robbed at the Union Hotel, Saratoga, of pearls valued at $20,000. There was a very fashionable lady, whose manners were exquisite, dress divine, and whose *tout ensemble* made a great impression on the susceptible Mrs. Wright. It is known that some women mesmerise others of their sex as much as they do men. As a matter of course she became intimate with Mrs. Wright—so much so that she frequented the room of Mrs. Wright very often. In this way she discovered the whereabouts of the trinkets and jewels, and while Mrs. Wright was absent from her room, listening to the music of the band attached to the hotel, the lady thief entered her apartment and abstracted the valuables from her bureau. About the same time the elegantly dressed lady left the hotel, and no clue to her whereabouts has been ascertained. From circumstances connected with the affair, and things that have since transpired, it appears the lady, who was introduced without reference to her character or antecedents, was accompanied to Saratoga, some days before the robbery, by a gentleman, who took board at another hotel."

"A man named Gilbert committed suicide in Prescott, Massachusetts, in a very singular manner. He managed to raise a piece of rock, weighing nearly a ton, about five feet from the ground; he then got under it, pulled the support away, and was crushed to death."

"On last Monday forenoon, as the St. John steamer 'Eastern City' was on her passage from this city to Portland, she ran upon a whale, knocking off her forefoot and causing a slight leak. At that time the vessel was about ten miles N.N.E. of Thatcher's Island, and was going at her usual speed. A school of five whales was in sight playing about, when suddenly one of them rose just forward of the bows, and was struck on the side, about two-thirds of the way back from the head, causing quite a shock to the vessel. The whale dove instantly, and not being seen again, was supposed to be killed. It was a large whale, judged by those who saw it to be seventy-five feet long. A few minutes after another whale was seen coming toward the vessel at great speed, and it was expected that the creature would attack the steamer, but at about two lengths distance it suddenly dove and disappeared. As the boat was on her return trip, this side of Portland, between Boon Island and Cape Elizabeth, she came near running upon another whale, but the creature dove at a distance of about ten feet from the vessel."

"Vermont appears to be rising in the Benician scale. At Brighton, Northern Vermont, Australian Kelly and Kerrigan had their set-to on Tuesday. The farmers furnished horses and wagons to convey the pugilists and their friends to the scene of combat. A farmer furnished a smooth meadow for the battle-field, and brought out scythes and rakes to prepare a suitable arena. The selectmen were present to preserve order, the high sheriff of the county drove down the stakes, and several members of the grand jury stood by to see that there was fair play, while the good lady of the farmhouse brought out every chair she had for the umpires, referee and reporters. They all had a good time. Kerrigan and Kelly fought a good fight, which resulted in favor of the former at the twenty-fifth round by a foul blow from Kelly, and the hospitable farmer's wife was made happy by a contribution of fifteen dollars. We hear of no disorder, no bloody fight with ambitious policemen, and no difficulty of any kind. The combatants had a fair fight, though it had, accidentally, a foul termination; and the good people of the favored rural district, who enjoyed both the sport and the dollars for their teams, are just as well off as if they had made a rumpus themselves."

"Rev. D. C. Mitchell is a revival Methodist minister, who has been preaching of late in West Stockbridge, Mass. Last year he preached in South Lee, and, while there, became more attentive to a young girl, named Webster, than to Mrs. M. or the little M.s. This, of course, occasioned some gossip, but as there was no proof of criminal intimacy, the Rev. D. C. had no difficulty in getting a new appointment from the Conference last spring. Lately, however, the guilty nature of the intimacy has become apparent, and he has been deposed from the ministry. A civil suit still awaits him, and it is to be hoped that justice will be meted out to this reverend rascal, and that parents will learn that ministers are no better than other men."

"La Mountain, the balloonist, met with a serious accident on his recent voyage from Albany. He travelled thirty miles in twenty-nine minutes, and in attempting to land at East Lanesboro, Mass., was caught in a tornado, and dashed against a stone wall, knocking him senseless, but breaking no bones. The basket rebounded, and was elevated to an equal altitude with the balloon, thus clearing the wall. It was then dragged along the ground at a fearful speed, and coming in contact with a tree, stripped it of its branches, and tore the network of the balloon to atoms. It continued its course some distance, when it came in contact with another tree, throwing Mr. La Mountain out, causing the balloon to collapse, and tearing it to tatters. Mr. La Mountain was not conscious for near half an hour, when he was found on the top of a mountain by some men, who had witnessed his perilous descent. He was very badly bruised and cut, but not so seriously injured as to prevent his riding to a farmer's house, where he remained twenty-four hours, when he returned to Lansingburgh, reaching home last night. His escape from instant death was most miraculous, as the balloon was driving along at the rate of a mile a minute when he was dashed against the stone wall."

"Another disaster is reported, resulting from the late storm. On Thursday last the schooner "Neptune's Bride," belonging to Gloucester, was lost on Malcolm's Ledge, between Seal Island and the Wooden Ball off the Maine coast. In attempting to land in a boat, the captain and eleven men were lost in the surf, and of two who remained on board one was washed off and drowned. The schooner was a total loss."

"The promised race between Flora Temple, the 'Queen of the Turf,' and George M. Patchin, the fastest trotting stallion known to exist, took place at the Franklin Trotting Park, on Tuesday afternoon, in the presence of an assemblage of horse fanciers and sporting men such as was never before witnessed in this vicinity on a similar occasion. The horses were induced to pit their respective qualities against each other by the offer of a purse of $1500, the race to be mile heats, best three in five to harness.

"The announcement of the race drew together about fifteen thousand persons from all parts of New England, who commenced pouring into the park several hours before the hour appointed for the trot.

"It was a very exciting race, and the fourth and last heat is thus described by the Boston *Journal:*

" 'By this time "the shadows of night were coming down fast," and the crowd had materially diminished. It was growing dark, and the horses could scarcely be distinguished across the course. The remaining spectators were becoming impatient, and fears were entertained that the race would not be concluded. But the irrevocable "Go" was uttered, and away went the steeds, Flora one length behind when they left the stand. Now they are side by side, now pacing through the darkness.

It could just be discerned that Patchen broke, and being set down again by his driver, made a close brush with the mare. The horses are not seen with distinctness until the huzzas of the multitude announce their near approach to the end of the race. A scene of intense excitement ensues, and amidst cries of "clear the track!" the horses sweep by the Judges' stand, Flora winning the heat and race in 2 28½.'"

"A meeting of the Bar of Massachusetts was held yesterday forenoon to consider the resignation of Chief Justice Shaw. A complimentary address to Judge Shaw, prepared by G. T. Curtis, was approved by the meeting, and a committee of one from each court appointed to present it. In place of Judge Bigelow, who has been appointed Chief Justice, Reuben A. Chapman, of Springfield, has been nominated by Governor Banks as Associate Justice of the Supreme Court."

"A daring attempt to rob the Providence Bank was made last week. Two young men went in and inquired for Mr. Dunne, the cashier. At the same time one of them dashed some spirits of ammonia into the clerk's face, but the brave youth kept them at bay with a chair, although partially blinded with the effects of the ammonia, and cried lustily for aid. The two thieves thereupon escaped, but were pursued and finally captured."

"Miss Tucker, the daughter of the popular and respected conductor on the Maine and Boston Railroad, was thrown from her horse lately and seriously injured."

"A double meteor, of rare brilliancy, was seen in many places in Boston and vicinity, on Friday night, about 10 o'clock—two distinct balls of fire, passing from the southwest toward the northeast, keeping within the same distance of each other during the whole time they were visible. They passed across the heavens with less descent than is usual with such luminous bodies. The light was so great that we hear of persons who rose from bed, thinking there was a fire nearby. Hundreds witnessed this novel spectacle in Boston, and we hear accounts of the meteors from Cambridge, Newton, Nahant and other towns.

"The Providence *Journal* gives the following account of this meteor:

" 'A most remarkable meteor was seen on Friday evening, about two or three minutes before ten o'clock. Its direction was from the west to the southeast. It appeared to be double, and to pass in a direction nearly parallel with the horizon, and elevated about 35 or 40 degrees above it. An observer who was in Hope Street at the time, saw it explode when nearly south of him, and he describes it as emitting for a moment a brilliant, greenish light, strong enough to cast shadows in the street.' "

"There have been more poisonings reported this week, by strychnine—and the details are very interesting, as well as very shocking. Two sisters, named Tirrell, died suddenly and mysteriously at Weymouth, in Massachusetts, and suspicion of foul play was no sooner awakened, than it found a criminal to fit it. It appears that one George Canning Hersey, a young mechanic of Weymouth, became intimate in the family of a Mr. Tirrell, and formed an attachment for one of the daughters, Mary Tirrell. This young lady died very suddenly in January last; but no suspicion of foul play arose at that time. On the 2d of this month, however, another daughter of Mr. Tirrell, Betsey Frances, died quite as suddenly, under circumstances which at once indicated strychnine as the immediate cause of her disease. Upon a post mortem examination, the presence of this deadly poison was clearly detected in the stomach, and the further discovery was made that the unfortunate young lady was *enceinte* at the time of her death. This led to the suspicion that the first victim might have died from poison also, and upon exhuming the body of Mary Tirrell, a quantity of corrosive sublimate was found in the viscera, and the fact was brought to light that she too had been *enceinte*. The investigation is still proceeding, and there is no doubt that the truth will soon show itself by the discovery of the murderer."

"The Musical Festival in honor of the Prince of Wales, at the Music Hall, Boston, on Thursday morning, October 18, in which school children participated, brought before the rising generation an event of deep significance. It might be termed an allegory in which they were actors as well as spectators. The children were ranged in four triangular rows of seats, all verging towards a common centre —the boys on the inside, and the girls on the outside, the dark clothing of the former making a background to relieve and display the brilliant toilets of the myriad buds of Boston Beauty.

"A platform was erected for the guests, while the spacious hall was densely packed with the maturer beauty and intellect of the Modern Athens. On this platform, and scattered around the Prince and his suite, were names illustrious in both hemispheres for their genius and reputation. We need only mention Everett, Hilliard, Agassiz, Emerson, Sumner,

Winthrop, Holmes, Longfellow, Fields, and some others of the most prominent poets, orators, philosophers and poetasters who have made Boston the hub-bub of the Universe. It was in truth a splendid sight, and one that must have deeply impressed the Prince and Duke as to the great importance paid to education in this Republic. Close to this band of Singing Birds and Philosophers were the New York reporters, who dressed in their best, cut a very imposing figure. Mr. Hamlin, the candidate for Republican honors, was also present, and seemed heartily to enjoy a scene so infinitely superior to the vivas of a mob. When the Prince had acknowledged the applause which greeted his entrance, and exchanged salutations with some of the most illustrious Bostonians around him, Carl Serraha, the leader of the orchestra, gave the signal, whereupon the Prince and the entire audience rose while the following appropriate ode, by Oliver Wendell Holmes, was sung:

"God bless our Fathers' Land,
Keep her in heart and hand
   One with our own!
From all her foes defend,
Be her brave people's friend,
On all her realms descend,
   Protect her throne!

"Father, with loving care,
Guard Thou her kingdom's Heir,
Guide all his ways;
Thine arm his shelter be,
From him by land and sea
Bid storm and danger flee;
Prolong his days!

"Lord, let War's tempest cease,
Fold the whole earth in peace
Under Thy wings!
Make all Thy nations one,
All hearts beneath the sun,
Till Thou shalt reign alone,
Great King of Kings!

"The remainder of the following programme was then performed in most perfect style:

"I. *Jubilee Overture*, by Von Weber, having for its theme the national air, 'God Save the King.'

"II. *Choral from St. Paul*, by Mendelssohn, with full orchestral accompaniment.

"III. 'Allegretto' from the *Eighth Symphony* of Beethoven.

"IV. 'Gloria in Excelsis Deo' from Mozart's *Twelfth Mass*.

"V. 'Andante' from the *Fifth Symphony* of Beethoven.

"VI. 'The Old Hundredth Psalm.'

"The entertainment lasted just one hour, and was very enjoyable. The Prince and party joined heartily in the applause and in singing the 'Old Hundred.' "

"A few minutes after ten the Prince arrived [at the grand ball at Boston in honor of the Prince of Wales] and was received by Mayor Lincoln in the reception-room. He was then conducted to the royal box, where he remained a short time contemplating the brilliant and exciting scene. Here a little contretemps occurred. Everybody crowding around him to speak to him, a vase of flowers was thrown down and covered the Prince with their fragrant fragilities. The clumsy courtiers who had caused the mischief were profuse in their apologies, but the Prince laughed so heartily at the accident that they themselves joined in the merriment.

"After remaining a few minutes the Prince descended to the floor, and did not return again to his box during the whole evening. But the box was by no means empty, for shortly after it was taken possession of by an elderly lady, who was accompanied by an advertising agent, who exhibited themselves to the public for two hours, and shocked the sense of decency of the entire company. It was like sticking a show bill upon the steps of the sacred altar. The way this distinguished party obtained possession of the deserted box was, we understand, through a gross breach of etiquette. The lady attacked the Prince, who was standing up for a quadrille, and coolly asked him to conduct her to his box. The Prince, with perfect good breeding (wonderful indeed under the circumstances), excused himself on the plea that he could not with propriety desert his partner. But the lady was not to be put off so, and asked if she might go herself to the box, to which the Prince of course bowed assent. That is the way, we understand from a gentleman who was standing close to the Prince at the time, that the distinguished lady, accompanied by the advertising agent, got possession of the Prince's box."

"Where the toilettes were all so superb [at the Prince of Wales' ball in Boston] and the ladies so numerous—over sixteen hundred being present—it seems almost invidious to particularise. But as our lady readers will demand some information on that most interesting subject, we select a few of the most distinguished toilettes for description:

"Mrs. Governor Banks attracted great attention. She was attired in a rich, heavy purple, figured in gold, which produced quite a brilliant effect. The waist was made low neck, with short sleeves, trimmed with point lace, and partially covered with a point lace bertha; the latter was beaded with a small gold braid. The waist was trimmed with gold. Diamond earrings and a head-dress of white feathers, with a heavy purple bow at the back, added much to the effect of her toilette.

"Mrs. T. E. Chickering was superbly attired. She wore a dress of mauve color and white tarletan, trimmed with point lace. The waist was trimmed across the front with mauve colored tarletan and with point lace. An elegant trimming of foliage extended down on either side on the front part of the skirt. The other trimmings were 'snow ball.' Her head-dress corresponded with the trimmings on the dress, being composed of green, white and gold. She wore a most valuable necklace of diamonds, and also earrings and a bracelet of diamonds. The diamonds were all of the finest water, and the whole toilette was equal if not superior to anything of the kind we noticed. She was the centre of considerable attraction.

"Miss Martha Haines Butt, A.M., the talented and accomplished literary belle of Norfolk, Virginia, the authoress of *Leisure Moments*, and the contributor of several highly popular pieces to the serial publications of the day, made an elegant appearance. She was attired in a rich white silk dress, with lace over-dress, the body with deep points, the dress looped with mauve Imperatrice ribbons, and studded at intervals with enamelled flowers of same color, bordered with gold; bertha of lace, ribbon and flowers to correspond with skirt. Hair braided in massive Grecian braids and decorated with white flowers and pearls. This dress was an exact fac-simile of one worn by the Empress Eugenie on a recent occasion. Miss Butt had a very elegant bouquet of New York manufacture, from the floral depot of Chevalier and Brower, 523 Broadway, under the St. Nicholas Hotel. It represented an imperial star, and was composed of blush rosebuds, tuberoses, heartsease, acanthus and sweet alyssum; it was supported by an elegant silver holder, ornamented with a deep white silk fringe. Miss Butt attracted much attention for her admirable figure, her exquisite costume, and for her graceful movements in the dance.

"Mrs. John L. Gardner wore a most elegant green moire antique, trimmed with point lace and green satin ruches. She also had on a costly bertha, a green velvet head-dress, diamond necklace and earrings to match."

"A man in Burlington, Vermont, offers 'hams and cigars, smoked and unsmoked, for sale.' "